A Boy In That Situation

A Boy In
That Situation

An Autobiography
by Charles Hannam

HARPER & ROW, PUBLISHERS
New York, Hagerstown, San Francisco, London

*The events described in this book are as true
as the author's memory allows, but a number
of names have been changed.*

A BOY IN THAT SITUATION: An Autobiography

Copyright © 1977 by Charles Hannam

Preface copyright © 1978 by Charles Hannam

FIRST AMERICAN EDITION

Library of Congress Cataloging in Publication Data
Hannam, Charles.
    A boy in that situation.

    First published in 1977 under title: A boy in your
situation.
    SUMMARY: The author describes his growing-up years
as a Jew in Nazi Germany and his subsequent life at school in
England.
    1. Hannam, Charles.   2. Jews in Germany—Biography.
3. Jews in Germany—History—1933–1945.   4. High
school students—Great Britain—Biography.   5. Germany
—Biography.   [1. Hannam, Charles.   2. Jews in
Germany—History—1933–1945.   3. Jews in England]
I. Title.
DS135.G5H34 1977b   943'.004'924 [B] [92]   77-11857
ISBN 0–06–022218–2

FOR PAM AND DAVID,
SIMON AND TOBY

Growing Up in Nazi Germany

The world I grew up in seems so remote now. It is so far away that it seems unreal. But it was real, and as I sat down to write this book it all came back. I had to face up to some personal facts: I had not been a very nice boy—though I suspect very few boys really are. I stole, I lied and I tried to forge my father's signature on a school report—not very skilfully, but I tried hard!

The *difference* between my family and so many others was that we were Jewish—trying to go on living in Germany in the 1930's when Hitler and the Nazis were coming to power. At the time I barely understood what was happening. Awareness that our religion was hateful to the government and to some of the German people only came to me gradually. I have since learnt a great deal about religious and racial persecution: It not only damages and blights the persecuted, it harms those who persecute—the persecutors lose their sense of humanity and justice, while the victims learn to hate themselves. At that time many of us German Jews began to believe some of the Nazi propaganda and to think of ourselves as ugly and unworthy. We would make jokes about our appearance and our occupations even though we had previously thought of ourselves as German more than Jewish. Now, this self-hate is not unique to Jews. There have been black children who suffered from discrimination and persecution and who began to believe that they were not beautiful and talented, and I am told that some Navaho youngsters watching a Western film cheered the cowboys rather than their own people, who were being slaughtered. At any rate, the Nazi myth of racial purity was accepted by some German Jews to an extent, and we would comment on hooked noses and black, curly hair with the same sort of disparagement as the Nazis did.

I suspect that most children are teased; it may be because they are thin or fat, clever or stupid, fair or red-haired. They hate it but in time the teasing stops, leaving some secret wound. But being teased for being Jewish was physically dangerous in the Germany of the 1930's. If I had not caught the train to England in May 1939, I would have been on one going to the Nazi death camps with millions of other Jews. Several members of my family perished, and I know now that for me it was a near thing. So what appeared at the start as malicious teasing by some boys and a few teachers ended in a deadly serious way. It was a preparation for their indifference to the fate of the Jews, and it laid the foundation for genocide. I have learnt since that unreasoning prejudice against *any* minority group can lead to such death and destruction.

By sitting down and remembering my childhood I have learnt many other things about myself: that I had suppressed a deep grief when my mother died and that she must have been a very spirited and humourous woman; that my father was a very calm and brave man who protected me from being afraid as much as he could; also that many of the non-Jewish people of Germany were good and decent—not all of them approved of the brutality and misery which in the end they were unable to stop. Most of all I have learnt that racial prejudice damages both the victim and the persecutor—it has not stopped, only the victims have changed. Big events have small beginnings; what happened to me is a small detail of the great catastrophe which in the end wiped out most of German and European Jewry.

Charles Hannam
Bristol 1977

Chapter 1

He was sitting up in his bed with brass knobs, a huge double bed really, when his father came in. He had the special look and he knew that something very serious had happened; so he made the right face too. He was eight and he knew that this was serious business.

'Hitler has got in,' said his father, and he didn't look excited or anything, just anxious, and he wanted Karl to know.

Normally at bedtime there would have been a good fight. Father had this trick – he would catch Karl between his legs and he would hold on ever so tight and even if Karl pushed and wriggled it made no difference. Father had got such strong legs because he used to ride horses, Mutti said. Karl and his sister, like other German children usually called their mother Mutti. There was this romantic story that he had courted her, no – she had first noticed him – because he rode past her house on a horse. It was probably a true story because there was a book on horse illnesses on the bookshelf in the drawing room. Anyhow at this moment, nothing like a good fight, just Hitler had got in and his father was serious about it and that was the end of the conversation.

He went out after the goodnight kiss and Karl had to do something special. So he put all the bedclothes over the end of the bed – it was a huge sack full of feathers in a sort of coverlet – and that was the horse. He then put on his red dressing gown and pulled the belt tight round his middle. That was important because not only did it look like a uniform but Karl thought it made him look thin; it would have been marvellous to be thin and military looking. Then he stuck his revolver into the belt and got out the broken air gun which had belonged to a cousin who had graciously passed it on – not much of a gun any more, it collapsed if it was held out, because the joint was broken. When the gun was still in good shape it had caught a visiting cousin, Helmuth, in the hand, the bit between the thumb and the first finger; he was led away, sobbing, and he never came again. The revolver was better stuff. It was black, and had been a starter pistol. Finally he put a dagger in his belt and mounted the 'horse' at the end of the bed.

The good thing was that all this was opposite a mirror in a wardrobe and he could watch himself on the horse on his death defying ride, falling off when shot. On special occasions he would cover his face with blood, with a bandage at a heroic angle like the film actor. The blood was actually mouthwash stuff that tasted of peppermint, but was slightly red. Karl was not allowed toothpaste any more since he had discovered that if you hit the end of the tube hard the paste would fly out a great distance, like a bullet from a gun. The mad ride began, deep-throat grunts of pain, and shouts of 'Uri, Uri . . .' Karl had seen a film in which the Swiss stormed the castle shouting that, and went on despite casualties and having their ladders turned over. The ride went on until he threw himself off the horse in a dead exhausted faint, rolling on his arm, and in his nose the smell of peppermint blood.

Karl had a room on the third floor of the house. There had been a nanny once but now there was just a succession of maids who would not stay because the children were so awful. They hated every new one that came.

Karl had really loved his nanny, Malli. Malli had been nice to Karl, played games with him and had listened to his stories – then suddenly she said 'I am going to get married', and Karl had rushed at her and pushed her hard against a door knob and she had been led away to her room and he to his. He never knew whether he had hurt her really or whether she was just pretending. Grown-ups did this sometimes, they tried to frighten him by pretending to be hurt and then they would look out from under their hands and laugh or sneer. Anyhow it seemed that Malli was going to marry a man who worked in an office at Krupps. Karl was furious and jealous and he hated the husband and he wanted Malli to stay, but no one took seriously how he felt. When he had pushed her against the door knob everyone thought that it was just naughty and his mother had told him to stand in a corner. He didn't stay there long but crawled under his bed. There was a lot of room there and no one really bothered with him when he went there. He kept on asking Malli why she was going to marry, why did she want to, and she just laughed and said 'grown-up people get married' and then 'it's a secret', and he climbed on to her. She had warm starchy aprons that felt cool and he wanted to know the 'secret' and she wouldn't tell, nor would anyone else – except Heini Rademacher. He said that two people sat close together on the bog and it was called fucking and that was it. Karl wasn't sure, but that was the best information he could get at that point.

Heini came from poor people. Poor people worked; and Heini's father came every morning and stoked the boiler. There were two noises first thing in the morning: the first was when the maids opened the shutters. They were roller shutters and had to be pulled up and it was quite hard work. The straps were made of canvas and had red and green on them and Karl couldn't quite pull them up by himself. The boilers were stoked next. Mr Rademacher came in through the bottom entrance which led straight to the boilers. He raked out the clinker in huge red pieces with bubble holes all over them. Once Karl had pissed on a piece which he had teased out of the boiler by himself – there was thick steam and a foul smell. Then Mr Rademacher shovelled on the coke that lay there in huge mountains. That was the next noise after the riddling.

Then the new children's maid would wake up Karl. That is he was already awake but pretended to be asleep just to make it a bit worse for her. The one with the family now was treated to a particular kind of baby talk – it came from a book called *Helen's Children* and there was this awful boy, Teddy, who turned a plate with soup in it over to see the tortoise underneath.

Karl copied his baby talk and said to the maid 'You are only here cos we solly for yo pore fing' and she was upset about this and cried and reported Karl to his mother.

She said that he must have picked it up from someone else because no child could have ideas like that, and she would tell her boy friend who was in the Hitler Youth. Karl was frightened because he knew the baby talk was daft and he did not want anyone to know that he was talking baby talk, except to her, and then it was only to annoy her anyhow.

Annoying nannies was a birthright – he had been told that when he was only one and a half he had annoyed a nanny by just saying 'hop gain' again and again until she shouted and said she had been a nanny to the Krupp children and she wasn't going to be treated like that. That was repeated as if he remembered saying it and in the end he did remember and repeated the story, and this somehow gave him permission to tease nannies and maids – except for Malli and she had gone off with that clerk at Krupps.

'You will come and visit me,' she had said and he had visited her one Christmas and she and that husband had hugged each other. Karl again asked what the secret was and she wouldn't tell him and she hardly ever came to the house after that.

The only time Karl and his sister worked together was when they tried to get rid of new nannies. One went because they had put vaseline on her toothbrush and a vacuum cleaner in her bed. She had marks on her face and she smelt funny, not of nice soap like the children had but pungent sweet-smelling soap. Other maids could be teased in different ways: there was undoing the bow on the back of the apron, that was routine stuff, just done in passing. Then there was sliding on the lino. On the second floor there was an area just covered with lino, all blue and slippery, and the maids polished it with electric polishers every morning and then Karl would slide over it. They wouldn't get really angry, just shout and then laugh or sometimes they would rub a wet flannel or something into his face. Their hands were red and smelt of a soap that came in large yellow pieces. Karl knew he would get away with it because he could sense they were not exactly afraid of him but they knew that they couldn't go too far with the little master.

The children had breakfast in the kitchen and then went off to school. It was a long walk and Karl had two satchels. One was for the slate and the books. The slate was grey and had a sponge hanging from it, and when Karl had written something on one side of the slate, he turned to the other side, and finally wiped it all clean with the little sponge. When the sponge got dry Karl spat on it, and when there wasn't much spit it spread chalk dust all over the slate. Then there was another little satchel for the morning snack – two rolls with liver sausage or ham in them.

The ham was important; there were always some remarks like 'it isn't really ham – it's kosher ham'. To eat or not eat ham had obviously been an important decision for the family. The parents had decided to drop that superstition but they didn't have the heart to tell Grandmother Hartland. When the family went to see her everything was as it should be: two kitchens – one for meaty things and the other for milky things, and if the maid or anyone touched the wrong food the knife had to be purified by being stuck into earth and there were special prayers.

The school Karl went to was a Jewish school. It was a huge red building with bare concrete steps and it was divided down the middle. The other half was for Protestant children. They were let out at different times so that there would not be any fighting.

On his first day at school Karl had lost his coat and he had cried, and in the lavatory someone had pushed him against the wet, green slimy wall and his hands had felt the wet slime and the moss. He cried until his mother found him and looked for his coat. At school they had given him sweets – because it was his first day – and some of the older boys had come into the classroom dressed in brown costumes and they had sung something about little dwarfs and about the dwarfs doing all the work. Later he had been given another paper bag, with green and gold spots on and frills at the end. It was so big he could only just get his arm round it and it had sweets in it as well. His mother had brought it back for after school.

Then he went to the grandparents that were her parents who lived near by in Bismarck Street. Their house was in a row with other houses, had a big iron gate and was dark and close inside. He was taken up to the breakfast room. There was a small lift from the kitchen up to this room. It was like a box, and if he had dared he could probably have sat in the box and let himself down to the kitchen to frighten the cook. In the breakfast room there was a turntable on the table. It had all sorts of dishes on it: for butter, ham, sausage, pastries, rolls, jam, and a big pot of coffee. You could turn the table round and round but when you did someone would always get angry.

Mutti's parents did not bother about diet laws at all but they too had a special voice for ham. Grandpa owned a big department store in the middle of the town. It was said in reverent tones that it was the most expensive store in the town and it was the first to have an electric escalator – that was said every time the store was mentioned. Grandpa had a pointed beard on his chin, a curly moustache, and his head was shaved and shiny. When the hair grew to tiny stubs Karl would tell him to have the flies' legs cut off and he would go and have his hair cut off completely again. He had a big round stomach and from it hung a watch chain made of gold and a very special watch. He would open the back for Karl to see the bits moving. Something was written inside the back with a fine flowing engraved writing. Also on that chain were tiny gold scissors, and a champagne swizzle-stick that was for swishing round and round so that the bubbles wouldn't go up your nose and make you burp. Karl, who thought that the bubbles were the best bit in lemonade, never understood that one. Then there was a little gold knife with a steel blade for cutting string. Grandpa had been trained as an assistant in the shop and the one thing he was really proud of was the way he could wrap a parcel. When he had finished, it was perfect and there was a little loop for carrying the parcel.

Karl was afraid of his mother's mother, Grandmother Freudenberg. She had black eyes and black hair, and her mouth drooped and she had big heavy bags under her eyes and she was always frightened – wouldn't let the children out of her sight and was always telling them what was dangerous. Don't eat fruit and drink water afterwards or you will get cholera. Don't ever buy ice cream from little vans or men on bicycles because it has typhoid in it. Don't make a noise. Don't get run over. Don't eat so much and you're not eating enough. She looked worried and unhappy all the time and she hated dirt. Karl was never allowed near her when he was dirty. Mr Rademacher had an allotment next to Karl's father's house in the Alfredstrasse, and one day Karl had helped him to manure the potatoes. The stuff came from the Rademacher cesspit and was pretty pure shit. When grandmother saw him she made him strip off on the veranda, and then told the maid to take him straight to the bathroom.

So, after his first day at school, Karl sat down, was told off for turning the turntable too much, given a ham roll and then asked what sort of day he had had. He couldn't tell even Grandmother Hartland about the mossy, pissy wall but his mother made her laugh when she told them about the lost coat. They said 'You won't forget this day'.

By the time Hitler came to power Karl had been to the school for years and now walked there on his own. It was a straight line from home down the road, only one bad crossing. (Later, when he was at the gymnasium, Max Amper went under a lorry on his bike so Karl wasn't allowed a bike and only learned to ride one when he was much older.) When he walked to his elementary school he went past the gymnasium, the one he was going to go to when he was eleven. It was grey and much bigger, and looked like a huge 'E' without the stroke in the middle. It had columns like a Greek temple over the entrance. Past the gymnasium was a wooden hut where they sold sweets and fizzy lemonade, red and green. The bottle had a glass marble in it and the man who sold Karl the lemonade had a spike and when he struck the spike in the neck of the bottle the marble went down and the green lemonade came out. There were also rolls with sausage in them and roll-mops in jars and rolls filled with raw meat, 'bifsteak tartare', in them. Never eat raw meat said Grandmother or you will get a disease in your bloodstream. The school was round the next corner after that.

On his first day at school Karl had drawn Easter eggs, all different ones, each one with a different decoration. Malli had already taught him to read and write but no one asked him at school if he could. Every one seemed particularly nice to him at the elementary school. They asked questions about the family: what is your daddy doing, I saw your daddy at the synagogue, are you going to be a banker like your daddy when you grow up?

One of the teachers, Mr Isaacs, had a boy who was supposed to be Karl's friend. Everyone always said *your* friend Manfred, *your* friend Alfred and they were not true friends. Manfred was weedy, had a hooked nose and thin fair hair. Karl always looked at noses: you could tell a Jew from the nose, and they all said how lucky he was not to have a Jewish nose. He tried to look into mirrors sideways to make sure that his nose wasn't crooked like Mr Isaacs. He went to tea there – tea was actually weak coffee, half rolls spread with marge and red jam. Karl was never allowed marge at home and it had a nice tangy salty taste. He had to nick it from the larder because marge was kept for the servants and the gardener.

'I bet you get better things at home,' said Mr Isaacs and then he asked what Karl had for lunch.

'Don't let people ask you a lot of questions,' his mother had always said to him. 'They want to know about us so they ask our children. Don't tell them anything.' That voice rose up and he muttered about what there had been for lunch that day. It had been boiled sausage and greens and cabbage mixed together; not very special but Mr Isaacs wanted to know what a Hartland had for lunch.

Although Mr Isaacs was nice to Karl he used to shout in the classroom. Three boys sat in one row and the plank they sat on was hinged. If anyone wanted to get out, they all had to stand up and fold the seat back. Once Karl had farted quietly when Mr Isaacs was near and he asked who had made that smell and no one owned up, so he made Karl and the other two boys stand up and he smelt them and Karl wasn't spotted. Another time Franz

Heimann, who was also his 'friend', reported him for pinching his leg and Karl was made to stand in a corner.

Franz had betrayed him, he had sneaked on him, but he still came to Karl's birthday parties. There was the time when he and Kurt Spiegel sat on Karl and Kurt said he was going to fart in his face, so Karl threw him off. There was cake on the table and they spent the whole afternoon fighting with the broken air gun. Late in the evening their mothers came to fetch them away.

Sometimes Karl was asked to tell stories to the class. This was what he was good at and he liked it when the teacher asked him to come out and tell a story. The stories came from a book he read at home and he just repeated them and no one ever said you have got all that out of a book. One story he read over and over again was about a puppet who had been bought by an Englishman, Mr Stobbs, and the puppet had the extraordinary gift of making faces and he could really frighten people. Once, when the butler came round with food at dinner, the puppet, Punch, made his deadman's face and the butler dropped the food and ran away shouting that he would never come back. It was a good feeling sitting on the teacher's desk telling a story while the others listened.

At the end of the term you got a report and in the elementary school it was always good. They all spoke well of Karl and the report was handed round the family and everyone smiled and each time it said 'praiseworthy effort' they all gloated over it.

School stopped at one and Karl walked back home. At the sweet-shop he would buy domino-shaped liquorice pastilles which he put on the back of his hand to lick them flat and make them bigger, and sweet balls that changed colour as they were sucked. The way back home was slow. There were the huge fat columns with advertisements to read pasted on them; the best were printed black on red paper and they were police announcements which described murders and other crimes. Karl came back to one of these again and again; it was about a man who had killed several people and there were pictures of the corpses wrapped in blankets. He could not see much of the corpse but the shape was there and he had one of his worst dreams about those sheets with human pieces in them.

There were other bad dreams and he spent a lot of his time protecting himself against them. One dream was heralded by a slow drum beat, and then his mother would advance towards him holding a coffin in her arms. What made it so awful was that the figure was white on black, like a reversed photograph, and she would come nearer and nearer and Karl would scream but not a sound would come out. Then he would look up and see his mother leaning over the bed and he would lie there out of breath, hoping that he would not go to sleep again for a long time. The best protection against that dream was to lie on his back because then he could not hear the drums in his ears.

Another dream he had was of being frightened by his sister who would lean over him laughing and pushing. The best protection against that dream was to fight his sister, to defeat her and to hit her back. His sister went to a girls' school; she had already passed through the elementary school and she did not seem to like Karl very much. He tried to avoid her but she would pinch him, call him 'fatty' and complain that he ate all the food and spoiled her things. Even worse than his sister were her friends, who ignored Karl and were grown-up and just took no notice of him, or they would laugh with his sister when she made jokes about him. He wanted to be noticed, to be allowed to play Monopoly with them or just to be talked to, but they wouldn't; and they went to dancing classes and they were allowed to go to the cinema more often than he was.

To get back to the advertisement columns, another thing he liked were the film advertisements. They promised such exciting things and there were two cinemas quite near the house, the posh one in the centre and the fleapit just before the tram stop where he got off for home. After reading the advertisements he had a choice of routes, either along the main street where the shops were, or along the back street which was quicker. It all depended a bit on how hungry he was and how much he had been told off for being late the day before.

Lunch was served in the sitting room. It was the room the

family spent the most time in. There was a large sofa for fighting on, Karl's toy cupboard, a big table where they all ate, and Mutti's cupboard where the sweets and her housekeeping money were kept locked. A cloth was laid on the table and Karl and his sister were put far enough apart so that they could not kick each other under the table. There was usually soup and then something hot for the main dish and after lunch sweets were distributed. They were bought in huge quantities, wholesale, and handed out after the meal. This way, Karl's parents said, the children would not eat inferior sorts of sweets and eating between meals would be cut out. They did not know that Karl bought sweets before and after school and they did not realise about the money that he stole.

There were several places where money could be found: in Father's night table, in the top drawer, there were several little tins; they had originally held indigestion tablets, but now there was one for each size of coin. Karl had learned to be careful not to take too many; he usually helped himself when he came in in the morning to give his father his good morning kiss. By that time Father was in the bathroom shaving. He used cut-throat razors and had one for each day of the week in little boxes marked with the day. When he shaved he had just his vest and his underpants on and he made marvellously funny faces when Karl came in. He pretended to grab Karl and get him covered all over with shaving cream and Karl tried to get hold of the shaving brush and to pretend he was shaving. He had tried privately once, but had left soap on the razor and been found out. After shaving Father put tonic on his head. His hair was very short and was parted on top. At this time Mutti might still be asleep or outside, and if she was Karl would quickly open the drawer and help himself to some money.

The other source was Mutti's drawer in the living room. That was tricky because he had to find the key in her handbag first, open the drawer and then shut it after he had taken a few pfennigs. The same key also opened the sweet cupboard, but that wasn't quite so urgent because Karl kept a store of sweets in his bedroom.

There was another drawer in the same sideboard that had a box in it full of medals: an Iron Cross second-class, a ruby studded half-moon, another cross, and a piece of metal strip covered with ribbon material. Then there was a flattened lead ball. All these had belonged to Uncle Eric. He was Mutti's brother and he had been a sergeant in the artillery in the first war. He had been in Salonica and had fought with the Turks and that was why he had the ruby studded half-moon. He had told Karl that the lead bullet had come out of a periscope which had been used for peering over the top of trenches. He had been shot at when using it one day. Eric was nice and funny but Karl didn't see him very often because he was running Grandpa's store in the town. When he came he always gave Karl toy soldiers but never ones that were wounded or dead. He wouldn't buy Karl a soldier who was on a stretcher carried by two others because he had seen too much of that sort of thing already. Eric was going bald and was bigger than most of the men in the family. His father had told Karl that Eric was called up in 1914 when he and Grandmother Freuden-berg were in Switzerland on holiday. Eric had to get his passport but it was in the safe and so he broke it open. Every day that he was away his family had canned his share of the dinner in special little tins and then soldered a three mark piece on the bottom of the tin and sent it to him at the front.

Karl's mother had become a nurse during the war and she had only got married to Father when the war was over. She had been a ward sister and then a theatre sister assisting a surgeon. She would not talk much about the war but she had a photograph album with lots of pictures of soldiers in it who had been in her care. One was a picture of a patient on a unicycle; he had been a circus artist and then, Mutti said quietly, 'We cut his leg off because he had blood poisoning'.

Father had been exempted from military service because his brother was serving in the army and he was allowed to stay be-hind to run the bank. His father, Karl's grandfather, had died when Father was quite young and so Father had been in charge of the bank ever since. Karl was not absolutely sure what the bank was about but of course it had something to do with money and everyone always teased him about how rich they were supposed to be.

'We are not as rich as all that,' his mother would say when he asked and then add, 'being rich is nothing to be ashamed of, and we aren't as rich as the other Hartlands anyhow.'

The second reminder about banking came on pocket-money day. As sweets were free Father thought the children should learn to save, and so on the first of the month both would meet in their parents' bedroom. There was a wall safe hidden in the wall behind the picture. The picture was an etching of a ship in a canal and it was just big enough to hide the square safe. Father took out a special big key and turned it in the lock several times. Karl had a yellow money box with the crest of the city of Essen on the outside. Four marks were put in the savings book. It was blue and had printed on the outside 'Levi Hartland'. He was Karl's great-grandfather and he had founded the bank. He had started as a butcher, Father said, had then become a weaver and then gone into the banking business. The bank had gone on for more than a hundred years. The pocket money was added up and at the end of every six months the interest was added. Father always explained how this was done and said to Karl, 'That is the sort of thing you have got to know.' He was always doing sums with Karl, at dinner he would suddenly ask 'What is seven times seven?'

After lunch in the living room the maid came in and cleared things away. Conversation always stopped when the maid came in and everyone sat silently, or else Karl's mother would ask the maid questions which had something to do with the house. After the sweets had been given out Karl would rag around with his father, sit on his knee, slip off and get caught between his legs; then his father would read the paper for a bit and then go to bed. He always went to bed in the afternoon, and Mutti stayed on the couch in the living room to have a sleep as well. She covered herself with Karl's furry baby blanket. It was silk, but made to look like fur. Karl would try to snuggle up and kiss her and if she said she wanted to have a sleep he would say 'What will you give me if I let you sleep?' and she would give him a small coin and he would go off and play with his soldiers in the hall.

There was a toy cupboard in the hall and the soldiers were kept in a cardboard box. There were several sorts and they were all precious to him. There was Frederick the Great on a horse. He had a three-cornered hat, and there were twelve grenadiers with high hats. One had a drum and another a flag. Most of the soldiers were from the Great War. The German ones were grey and the French bluish grey and their helmets had a ridge over the top. Then there were sections of trench with little poles stuck into the papier-mâché and thin wire to pretend it was barbed wire. There were also some soldiers with fatigue caps, one playing a harmonica, another drinking from a bottle. Those had been presents from Uncle Eric. Karl would build forts and castles and then listen anxiously for his sister who would come along and upset his walls or step on them.

After the quiet time Father would go back to the bank. He had a hat with a rim and a thick cane walking-stick with a silver knob on the top of the handle. He walked from the house to the tram stop (he had a season ticket) and then he went back to the bank. Karl had been born in the house where the bank was. His parents had lived there until he was three and then his father had sold a plot of land for a lot of money and they had bought the house they were in now. It was a ten minute tram ride away from the bank and it stood on its own. On one side there were allotments (the Rademachers had theirs there) and on the other side was a huge car park. Opposite the house was the tram terminus and the entrance to a large park and exhibition centre. So on public holidays the car park was often full of cars, and twice a balloon had taken off from there.

The house was surrounded by trees – 'the house in the woods'. Someone had said that and Karl wondered whether it was a joke or an insult. There was an iron entrance gate. At its side stood a willow, covered with a black spongy growth – a willow disease, they said. The drive led up to a simple portico and that was the proper entrance. Karl would often nip round the back, where there were steps up to a veranda which had been built round a tree. When the weather was good the family would eat outside.

When it was warm there were cold soups which Karl hated and he was very pleased when a bird shat into the soup bowl one day. Shit jokes were always all right in the family and everyone was rolling about laughing – 'But for God's sake don't tell Granny Freudenberg' said Mutti still laughing. That grandmother was thought to be particularly shockable and the children were warned not to be rude in front of her.

Grandmother Hartland, who was pious and kept the religious rules, was never discussed in that sort of way. She had kept the flat above the bank and Father used to visit her there every day and tell her how things were going. She had a small dog with silky white hair, and a canary. When she had an egg she used to take off the top and share it between the canary and the dog. Friday evening was her evening 'at home', and everyone went except Karl who they said was too young to go. He hated being left behind and made a big fuss. He asked what they had to eat and they said it was always chicken soup and chicken, and then Karl would burst into tears and when he was younger he puked as well. It was quite easy. He just put his finger into his throat and it would all come out in a gush. One day he had had spinach and pancakes and it all came out and they decided to leave him where he was – lying in the slime and the green with bits of pancake – and that was the last time he puked in his bed. He still made himself sick when he needed to be ill but never again in bed.

In the evening the family had supper in the proper dining room. That was a big room with parquet floors. The floor was rubbed down with spirit and wire wool once a year and Mrs Senft, who came for the rough cleaning, and several other women would join forces and scrub the floor. The whole house smelt of spirit and the supper was served upstairs. There was a big picture on one of the dining room walls – it was called 'The Bean-feast'. It was a Flemish feast and there was a man being sick at the table and the bean king with a crown on his head sat at the end of the table with his arm round a girl whose breasts were squeezed into her dress. Karl looked at the picture a lot because his seat was opposite it and he had his special napkin ring there. It was thin silver with tiny holes in it – 'You bit them when you were a baby,' said his mother. His sister sat opposite and glared at Karl. When the grown-ups weren't looking he would make faces at her and she would try to kick him. He knew how to annoy her. He would open his mouth wide with food in it, half-chewed, and show it to her, or he would slip whole butterballs into his mouth and she would shriek with horror and report him. The maids used to pat the butter into small balls between two little boards with serrated surfaces and there was a pile of these butterballs in the middle of the table. The parents went on with eating their own food, until suddenly there would be explosions of anger, when the children exceeded the permitted amount of aggression.

On Saturdays lunch was also served in the dining room and one Saturday the family had reached the stewed plums and a vanilla flavoured sauce when the phone rang. It was Pola Feuer, Grandmother Hartland's maid, saying that her mistress had just died of a stroke. Mutti had taken the message and she added that Grandma had had the stroke on the lavatory. Karl cried and went on eating his plums because he did not know what the right response to such news was. He had liked Grandma, although he had hated kissing her. She had long rough hairs on her cheek, but she had been kind and she had died.

Karl went to the graveyard where all the Hartland's were buried when his grandmother died

'That's Ludwig's grave,' said Father. Ludwig was his brother and he had died just after the war and had left two children and a wife behind. It was because of him their father didn't have to go into the army. 'That's Ida's and that's Helen's grave' – two sisters who had died after the war in the Spanish influenza epidemic. Father never talked about any of the family much, their relations came visiting but there was no warmth. Next to the grave-yard were a huge gasholder and factories and it took a long tram ride to get there.

There was another older Jewish graveyard where Levi Hart-land had been buried but that was full up and locked. Karl had just been able to see the Hebrew on the yellow stones when he went there once. Someone had climbed in and turned stones over and had marked them with stars of David and written 'Jew' with thick brush strokes in black. So thickly had the paint been put on that it had run down the edges.

After Grandma's death Mutti and a maid and Karl went to her flat to clear things out. The dog and the canary had already gone and the brass cage stood empty. Cooking pans stood all over the place; there were boxes full of old Hebrew books and glassware. Karl was rummaging in the drawers thinking how strange it was that he should be allowed to do it openly. He always went through drawers at home but only really to find money or to see what presents had been hidden away for his next birthday. He found a little glass rod with green bits of nose-pickings sticking on it.

'What's that?'

'Oh that's a nose-poker,' said his mother bursting into laughter, and Karl suddenly realised that she hadn't liked Grandmother Hartland very much and thought her to be odd and ridiculous, so he laughed too but also felt bad because it had been her nose-poker and he didn't really see why she didn't poke her nose with her fingers as everyone else did.

Karl went to the synagogue every Saturday. There was a session for children where he learnt Hebrew, and for the service he joined his mother on the upstairs balcony. This was a 'modern' or 'reformed' synagogue and the pride of the Jewish community. It had been built by an architect, Mendelson, and this was always mentioned in a specially reverent tone of voice. It was, Mutti said, built in the style of the Hagia Sophia in Constantinople, and she said that in the same sort of voice as she had talked about the nose-poker. The synagogue was magnificent, a monument to the wealth of the Jewish community and the Hartland banks must have made some contribution. There was a great organ, mosaics on the walls, and lots and lots of lights, electric lights, in the shape of candles, and Karl felt he was nearer to his god when he half shut his eyes and the lights flickered. Father had a seat in the front row. There were little lockers where prayer shawls and prayer books were kept. In the entrance hall was a cloakroom and when Father went in he handed in his hat, stick and coat and in return the lady gave him a leather box that had his top hat in it. The top hat was black and shiny and had a little velvet cushion at the bottom, and Father stroked it one way to make it look all shiny. He said in a reverent voice that it had come from England. He had spent a year in England as an apprentice and talked about the country as somewhere special where the food was mildly odd. He mentioned plum pudding and sharp sauces and he bought an English paper at the station occasionally.

There was a special service for the dead and Karl went to watch his father say the prayer for his grandmother. He and Karl came in when everyone was in his seat. The *warden* opened the door and everyone turned towards them as they walked slowly up to the front. Men came out from their pews to shake hands and to say they were sorry. The special prayer for the dead, the Kaddish, was said and a row of men muttered the prayer, 'yish kadal yish kadash', bending forward slightly as they were saying it.

When Grandmother Hartland had been dead a year a gravestone was put above her grave and above one of the doors in the synagogue a little plaque with her name on was fixed with an electric light with a blue bulb, and Father said the light would burn for ever.

Chapter 2

The time had come for Karl to move on to the secondary school and the family talked about it very naturally; it was just what was going to happen next. Cousin Joseph was already there, much senior, experienced and with signs of hair on his upper lip. He was the sister's friend and more or less ignored Karl but gave him old toys. Joseph's father had died after the war and Karl's father seemed to look after his brother's children. Occasionally Mutti had said Joseph was thick and that he needed extra lessons and that was thought to be a bit of a disgrace. What was much worse was not to be moved up at the end of the year. This disaster had happened to Uncle Eric, Mutti's brother. Father often referred to it but never when Eric was there. As if to cheer Karl up his mother said he wasn't to worry about staying behind because it could happen to the best of people and it had even happened to Bismarck. Joseph spoke about the school with ease and familiarity: 'Be careful if you get Old Ivan,' he said, 'he is called Old Ivan because of Ivan the Terrible, but the music master is nice and you will get Kosch as your form master.'

It was scary and confusing. The only good thing really was the caps. As Joseph explained: 'In the first year you have a blue cap with a gold stripe, in the second a gold and silver stripe and in the third two gold.' Each school had its own colour: the crown of the Goethe Gymnasium cap was blue for the first three years and then green, but that was so advanced it was beyond Karl's imagining.

His father had gone to a gymnasium in the centre of the town but he had left early to learn about banking, had gone to London and Paris and then had suddenly been recalled when his father had died. Father was full of classical tags and would shout them out so often that Karl knew them long before he actually knew Latin. His father also explained the tags. 'Timeo Danaos et dona ferentes' was about the Greeks and Trojans; and whenever he put money into a collection box he would say 'bis dat quis cito dat', and when there was wine it would be 'in vino veritas'.

There was a problem about the gymnasium for Karl; a Jewish quota had been introduced, only ten per cent of the children in the school were allowed to be Jewish. Karl went to the school with Father and they met Mr Karpf. He had fought in the war; you could see this by his buttonhole in which he wore a small bow made up of black and white silk with crossed metal swords on top. He had his son Ernst with him and Karl didn't like him at all. He had a huge nose – a 'typical Jewish nose' thought Karl – and he felt ashamed of his father because it was clear that he was asking for a favour from an official and wasn't quite sure of himself. Karl heard him say: 'My brother fought at the front and he died after the war; his son is already at the school.' The director of the school looked at Karl briefly and did not seem very interested. He asked what he read but did not listen to the answer. Karl wanted to tell him about the Greek myths; he knew that telling about the *Punch* stories would not go down nearly so well. Karl's father said something about paying the fees, of course, and then they all went away. Karl shook hands with the director, bringing his heels together smartly so that they made a clicking noise and bowing his head sharply from the neck downwards. He had been taught to be polite like this for a long time and visitors had often said: 'Doesn't he do his heel clicking nicely.' Karl knew that the director had to be shown that he was no mere Jewish boy, soft, with a big nose, but a hard and precise citizen.

A letter in a blue envelope came a few days afterwards. Karl had been admitted as a special case even though his father had not fought in the war. He felt ashamed for his father who had missed the opportunity for being heroic. To Karl heroic really meant riding at the end of the bed into the hail of bullets from French soldiers, keeling over and having one's forehead covered with a nice long scar and congealed blood. The only wounds Karl seemed to get were cuts on his knees, and then his mother would bandage him up and he would walk stiffly past his sister's friends, hoping that they would enquire how he had come to hurt himself, and he could then be brave about his wound. The one time he had hurt himself seriously was on the building site beyond the end of the garden. He had stepped into a fire that seemed to have gone out but something hot burnt his heel. He limped home and couldn't tell his mother because he thought she would be angry, so he confided in his sister who told him to stick his foot into water to cool it down. After the blister had burst a hole appeared and seemed to be getting deeper and deeper. And then his mother noticed, put yellow powder into the wound and bandaged it properly. Karl said he had knocked his foot on the end of his scooter and he was a bit surprised that his mother believed him. 'I am getting better at lying' he thought to himself, and he was, too.

He operated on two levels, lies that were found out and lies that were not found out. Whenever he *was* found out he would comfort himself that they had never found out the really bad things he had done. He was found out when he had broken the virginia creeper vine that covered most of the house with glorious foliage. When the leaves turned red in autumn everyone was 'ooing' and 'awing' and it was clearly thought to be an important part of the beauty of the house. The whole vine grew from a root in front of the kitchen, and one day Karl just stood on it and it cracked. Karl covered the crack with mud and went away. The next day all the leaves drooped and he could hear his parents talking about it in worried voices. They asked Karl, and of course he said he knew nothing about it, but then the gardener came and showed the parents the cracked branch and said: 'It was the boy, I saw him.' Karl felt his face going all red. He hated blushing and the more he blushed the more he hated it. His sister used to shout, 'I can see you are lying, you liar, because you are blushing, red as a beetroot.' Sometimes with the really big lies he managed not to blush; it was all luck, but he knew that he could get away with things as long as he didn't.

When the letter came from the school saying that he had been accepted he was taken to the hat shop to get his school cap; blue on top, with a shiny black peak and the first golden stripe. He wore it whenever he could, walking slowly past people, and they said, 'Look! He is going to the gymnasium and he has got a new cap. Watch out you don't get kept down to do the year again because then you will have to wear the same cap for two years.'

The Jewish quota at the school wasn't the only thing that made Karl realise that life was changing. Jewish shops had their windows smashed in; he saw them in the town centre. They had broken glass and stars of David painted with whitewash on the remains of the window. And even where the windows had not been smashed printed posters had been stuck on saying 'Germans defend yourselves, don't buy from Jews'. Usually this happened where the name of the shopkeeper was obviously Jewish. Karl was learning what were Jewish names and what were not. They were sometimes odd names like Rosenzweig or Herzberg, but most often common ones like Cohen.

Relatives always complimented Karl on his appearance: 'You don't look Jewish at all', 'What lovely fair hair', 'Blue eyes'. People would say of others, too, how non-Jewish they looked, or, on the other hand, how very Jewish. 'Typical, typical,' shouted Aunt Julia, Joseph's grandmother, when she saw the Hartland girl from the other branch of the family, the 'other Hartlands' as they were called. 'Just like a negro,' she muttered, 'thick lips, fuzzy hair and look at that nose.'

The other Hartlands were also bank owners, but they had gone ahead more vigorously than the firm of Levi Hartland and their bank had great Greek columns and many more clerks and telephones. The two brothers who ran that bank went about their business in huge cars – one grey, that was for brother Arnold, and one maroon, and that was for brother Kurt. Mutti used to snort about show-offs when they went past. Uncle Arnold, the one with the grey car had a boy who was the same age as Karl, and although the families did not have an awful lot to do with one another it was thought to be a good thing that Karl should visit him. Before long everyone referred to him as Karl's friend Lutz. Lutz was very thin, had enormous glasses and exuded anxiety and nervousness, all this in contrast to Karl who was fat and, it seemed to others, exuded good nature and friendliness. The big grey car used to call outside the Hartland house and Karl was taken to the other Hartlands to play.

Theirs was a Georgian style house by a lake, and they even had footmen and a butler and an English governess who shrieked 'daarling' at a rather defensive Karl. There was a garden so big that the boys never explored it all, but they disappeared in it and did as much mischief as two rather lonely and pampered boys can do in a single afternoon. In the Chinese garden they speared golden carp with a poker; they trampled on the flower beds; tried to sink the boat; and once Karl conveyed to Lutz his version of the facts of life, or rather Heini Rademacher's version. That evening when Karl was home the phone rang and there was a long conversation, but Karl did not really find out what it was all about. His mother said, 'What have you been up to? They can't get Lutz to go to sleep. He keeps on talking about your visit and has got a temperature.' Karl blushed but could not recall anything unusual. He had recited a verse he had heard at school:

> *This is Ernst Roehm's grave*
> *Like a cad he did behave*
> *He screwed so many SA bums*
> *With what should be reserved for mums.*

This had been during tea. They had 'English tea', which so far as Karl was concerned, meant there wasn't enough to eat, and he particularly disliked little white bread triangles. He had once told his mother the verse about Roehm, and she had shrieked with laughter. Even at the English tea party there was a good deal of laughter, particularly from Lutz's mother who seemed to like Karl and smiled at him with her wide round eyes. About her his mother had said, 'She is very ugly but when anyone is that rich people say she looks interesting.' So Karl kept on looking at her. He wasn't at all certain what the rhyme was about but it certainly made the grown-ups laugh and so he kept repeating it.

He had seen Roehm once. A party rally had been arranged next to the house on the large car park. The men all had motor bikes and black crash helmets and each bike had a side-car. They all stood neatly to attention and the whole car park was full of motor bikes. Karl saw it all over the wall and Roehm walked right by him, a red face with a big scar and a huge dagger by his side which he was holding so that it looked as if he was going to pull it out at any moment. He walked past all the men and then he finished the inspection and shouted *Heil Hitler* and they all yelled back *Sieg Heil* and there was an awful roar. Karl hid behind the wall at that moment. He thought, if they see me and if they know I am Jewish they will come over the wall and smash me up. But no one took the least notice of him. Karl's father told him shortly afterwards that Roehm had been shot and that it was good riddance. Then he added very earnestly, 'You must never tell anyone that I said that. What we say in this house is not for anyone else's ears and if anyone asks you questions you mustn't tell them anything.' This was said in such a way that Karl knew his father really meant it and he began for the first time to become aware of danger.

One day at lunch in the upstairs room Mutti announced, 'Grandfather and Grandmother Freudenberg are coming to live with us. They are going to have your room and you will move upstairs.' To Karl this was not a bad move. It meant a room all for himself away from his parents and sister; a room with an attic roof and a view of the allotment. On the other hand a change like that was disturbing and he asked why they were coming. 'The store has gone bust. They are bankrupt,' said his father and he spoke with feeling. The department store had not been able to stand up to the competition of other stores and the anti-Jewish boycott. Karl learned more as time went on by listening behind the door of the drawing room, or by pretending to play with toys whilst the adults were talking. As far as he could understand it his father thought that it was all Eric's fault, what with modernising the store at a time when money was short and all the nonsense about having the first electric escalator in Essen. And there was the added bitter thought of all the money they 'wasted on themselves with pretentious gestures'.

So the grandparents arrived and took over Karl's room. There were two huge mahogany beds and a couch in front of the bed for the little afternoon naps they liked to take. Karl once hid under the couch and when his grandfather, who Karl thought was always ready for a bit of fun, came in Karl shrieked, 'Boo hoo I am a monster.' Grandpa was clearly more frightened by this unprovoked attack than Karl had intended and Grandma Freudenberg went for him with an umbrella, calling him a little devil and shouting that he had frightened his grandfather to death. Karl was terrified and wet his pants, something that had not happened for many years. He was frightened and furious, but also so petrified that he couldn't move. 'It's all right,' said Grandfather, 'he didn't mean it and I have recovered.' Grandma didn't actually hit Karl but the umbrella only came down slowly, and Karl felt all cold and wet round his legs. He went to his room. 'Get washed and changed,' snapped Grandmother, and Karl muttered to himself that the old sow had made him piss his pants and he would get even with her.

In the room that used to be his there were now huge wardrobes with great mirrors, and inside were drawers and many different compartments. Karl had a good look when his grandparents were out. There were piles of shirts with stiff fronts, separate piles of collars and cuffs that could be buttoned to the shirt halfway up. 'Your grandfather looks as if he had just been peeled out of an egg,' his mother said, and it was true. Nothing was ever out of place on Grandfather. Grandmother's dresses had always been a legend, after all they had owned a fashionable store and the family had been smart dressers.

Over another smaller wardrobe hung a picture of 'little Ernst', as Grandmother used to call him. It was an enlargement of a photograph and it had been coloured by hand. He was lying on a silky rug, the same Mutti used to cover herself up with when she had her afternoon nap. The background of the photograph was blue, the rug golden and the child fair and pink. His head was raised up and he was lying on his stomach. Ernst had died in early childhood and Grandmother used to talk about him a lot. He was a beautiful boy, a gifted boy, surely a talented boy. Then he caught diphtheria and died. Karl felt jealous of him and wished there was someone in the world who would say such nice things about him. He listened to the same story about beautiful little Ernst again and again, and if he wanted to put his grandmother in a good mood he would ask her to tell him about little Ernst.

Another story she liked was about the village where she grew up. Grandfather used to tell that one, and to underline how simple life had been for her family he said they never ever had bread and jam and butter; it was either bread and butter or bread and jam, and it was black bread and not white bread either. When they had pieces of boiled sausage Grandfather would say, 'Let me show you how they ate sausage in Grandmother's village.' And then he would cut a piece off the sausage and put it on a piece of bread, and devour it, holding the sausage and the bread in both hands. No one was more refined than Grandmother Freudenberg now, the least speck of dust upset her; all the fruit had to be washed and she did not seem terribly amused by Grandfather's joke.

The new school, the gymnasium, was not a happy place. In the elementary school Karl had been somebody, a 'Hartland', someone who was known and possibly appreciated. After all he always brought more money than anyone if there was a collection for an outing or for a charity. 'Ah yes, the Hartlands have been generous to us,' said Mr Isaacs when Karl presented a three mark piece rather than the customary fifty pfennigs to be put into the cardboard box. The children grew vegetables on a little plot behind the school and one day Mr Isaacs held up two cabbages. 'Who is poor?' he asked, and Karl wanted to put his hand up because he hated the thought of anything free going anywhere else but to him. But he hesitated when he saw the hands that did go up. He knew these boys were poor because of the clothes they wore, the sandwiches they brought to school – no liver sausage on fresh white rolls for them but black bread, margarine and very red jam, or a thick black treacle which they said was made from beets. He tried this treacly jam at home once where there was always a supply for the servants, and his mother told him that was all they had had to eat in the war. The war always came up when food was discussed: it seemed that everyone who had anything to barter would take a train into the countryside. When they saw a farmer they offered him whatever they had – carpets, clocks, gold coins, or jewellery. In return they were given potatoes, butter, eggs or meat.

Karl went to his new school with his new cap and with his new gym kit: red trousers with a blue stripe and a gym vest with a big letter 'G' on the middle of the chest. He no longer carried school books in a bag strapped between his shoulders but had a leather bag. His sister had had one like that for years and carried it with a much practised slouch, either under her arm or swinging it in a circle. Her bag was dark with age and battered looking. Like his cap, his bag spelt novice and Karl was conscious of the superior looks the older boys gave him. 'New bug,' they muttered and one stepped on his new brown shoes. 'My mum says I should stamp on all brown beetles.'

In the classroom the new form teacher introduced himself. 'If you want to know anything or are in any sort of trouble come to me,' he said. He had hair cut very short and a little bit stood up like a brush, or perhaps like a handgrip to pull him out of the water if he was drowning. He wore a button with a swastika on it in his lapel buttonhole.

'I must now make up the register and get to know you all,' 'Hartland,' he said when he came to Karl. 'The banker? Are you Jewish?'

'Yes.'

33

'What a pity. I had hoped for a completely Aryan class. Oh well.'

The same conversation took place when another pupil, Ernst Karpf gave his name. Karl hated him, his big nose, his unheroic manner and the fact that his father worked in a bank as well, the bank that belonged to the other Hartlands. He felt sure that without this companion all would have been well and the Jewish quota cut to more manageable proportions.

The school was disturbing in a number of ways. The teachers came and went when a period ended; there were enormous staircases; and the hall, true to the tradition of Latin culture the school fostered, was called the 'aula'. Then there was homework, and on top of everything else Karl already realised that he was an outsider. 'You a Jew then?' one of the boys said during break.

Worst of all were the physical education lessons. They were taken by a thick-set man with a thick neck and huge muscles who wore a white gym vest. His pectoral muscles bulged and below them his stomach stuck out till it disappeared under his belt. One day Karl saw that he wore a corset with strings going crossways. It was creamy white and he felt quite ill when he saw it – it was a bit like seeing a huge scar or anything else one was not supposed to see. He had special gymnastic lessons with his sister on the lawn at home, gentle rhythmic stuff, balancing while the lady beat a tambourine. Karl remembered the feeling of excitement and horror when one of her tits slipped out of her loose gym costume. It was fascinating but she said 'Oh' and 'Look away, you bad boy.'

The gym lessons at school were grim because Karl could not do the things that he was supposed to do. The worst were the wooden bars which went to a giddy height, right up to the ceiling. There were thick ropes as well. 'Get up the ropes, you fat pig,' said the gym master. 'Get up or I will beat you till you do.' He supported the threat with a smart cut with a skipping rope on Karl's bottom. 'Get up, you fat pig,' chorussed Karl's class-mates, only too pleased to find someone who was useless. Karl strained at the slippery wooden bar but his hands would not pull him up and his legs were left dangling. Occasionally his feet would hit the bar where his laces went over his instep, which hurt a lot. There was one bony lad, tall, hair cut like the form master with a little tuft in front, his brown eyes glittering and alert. He was 'the best' in the class, answered questions first and somehow his answers were also ones that pleased the teachers. 'Jewish pig,' he hissed, 'you fat idle, Jewish pig, you can't do anything, you are useless.' There was much laughter and the only way out Karl could think of was to pretend that it was all a great act, a joke, done on purpose to make everyone laugh. It didn't work and he felt alone and miserable. The other area of special dread was a supple iron bar suspended between two upright bars. There was a box full of chalk and the ones who were good at gym rubbed the chalk on their hands to get a good grip and then swung about effortlessly, knee over the bar, turn, pull up and turn again. Karl hung from the bar. 'Pull yourself up, you lazy pile of fat.'

Now it was true that Karl was fat. The whole family was inclined to corpulence and the meals cooked lovingly and served regularly, the delicious rolls for mid-morning break, the sweets before and after school and the cakes bought to supplement the morning snack had produced results. The cakes were bought in the school basement. They were triangles of coconut and pastry and each corner was coated with chocolate. Karl also bought glasses of lemonade and felt a bit comforted. He hated being fat because he was teased everywhere. His sister got at him, his mother would put her hand lovingly on his to hold him back as he tried to grab yet another roll at supper, only Father and Grandfather could not say much because both carried big stomachs in front of them. 'A well set up man,' Grandmother would say admiringly. Being thin and muscular certainly was not part of the family ethos, but the other boys in the form felt they could take it out on 'fatty' who was also a Jew. The only advantage Karl had was that he was not as awful as Karpf. Karpf was just hopeless. Karl could be funny and sometimes made people laugh but Karpf just sweated and looked superior or frightened at alternate moments.

National economy and self-sufficiency were the big things at that time. We must not buy 'foreign' goods they said in school, we must raise our own pigs. To that end a big wooden bin was set up in the playground and each boy dutifully brought potato peelings, cabbage stalks and stale bread for the bin. Once or twice a week Karl would bring his load to show that he too wanted to help. One day as he approached the bin he saw his classmates in a cluster, they were sticking Karpf into the bin and when his head bobbed up they pushed him down again. Karl disappeared and locked himself in the lavatory until the end of the break, leaving his bag behind. In the classroom the boys were happy and excited. 'We tipped your mate into the pig bin,' they said and Karl wanted to say that Karpf was not his mate and that he would have liked to have tipped him into the bin as well, but the situation had *made* Karpf his mate, his fellow sufferer, and this was the worst thing he had to put up with. When the form master breezed in the boys shouted, 'We tipped the Yid into the pig bin, Sir,' They liked him, he was a friendly man, strict but fair. He nearly laughed, then pulled himself together.

'That was wrong. Hartland and Karpf leave the room.' The two crept out and waited in the corridor, not saying a thing to each other. 'He told us to be decent to you although you are Jews,' they said afterwards.

The school seemed an extraordinary place to Karl. Everything depended on quick, precise and smart answers. 'The capital of Greece?' 'Athens.' 'Right.' And the teacher would bring a thick notebook out of his pocket and enter a mark. There were two sets of marks, one lot for oral work and the other for written work and at the end of the term there were reports. Karl's parents waited anxiously for the report and indeed for any sign of success in school. Karl would often report good marks and they would say he was a good boy and at coffee time when his mother's friends were there to eat cream cakes and nourishing little salads Karl would be paraded before them and they would say, 'What will you do when you grow up, be a banker like your daddy?' Or they would admonish him to work hard because there was so much anti-semitism in the schools, and he must prove how good he was. When they asked if there was any trouble at his school he would say 'No' and they would say, 'We hear the Karpf boy has a bad time.' Karl would answer that he was a special case and they all agreed that the Karpfs were a bunch of stuck-up snobs.

Karl made one friend, Rudolph. He had a stick and walked awkwardly. 'Polio when I was a child,' he explained. Karl liked him because he never teased him and they walked home together. They talked about their families; they boasted to each other about their exploits and they gave each other some sort of support. With the money he took in increasing amounts from home Karl would treat Rudolph to cakes and sweets and Rudolph accepted because Karl came from a rich home and therefore had more money to spend.

The last report of the year coincided with Karl's birthday and he felt very nervous. He feared there would be no presents if the report was not a good one, and he knew it wouldn't be. The reports were handed out in envelopes and Karl tore his open in the lavatory. Every single mark was 'satisfactory' except physical education where, not unreasonably, there was an 'unsatisfactory'. At the bottom was one single remark, 'Precocious'. Karl did not quite know what his form master meant by that but he took the report home and if there was disappointment in the family it was not shown.

Karl felt quite guilty when magnificent presents were waiting for him. The best present was a black, plastic mac with a belt that he could pull tight. He had wanted it so very much and, as always, his mother had given him what he wanted most. When he was much smaller he had wanted a horn, a sheep's horn that had a metal squeaker on it. He had wanted it at the seaside for storming castles. Suddenly, like a miracle, the horn had appeared. And now it was the black, plastic mackintosh and he was going to take it on holiday and school was forgotten for the time being.

Chapter 3

By the time he had reached secondary school age, Karl and his sister were being sent to holiday homes for the summer. The first one was on Wyck, an island off Hamburg. They got there by train and ferry. The children were sent on their own and managed well enough. Once away from the adults they got on quite well. Possibly blood was thicker than water, or possibly they didn't have to compete for attention and love. In fact Karl became quite obedient and did what his sister told him to do. At home most of his ingenuity went on getting the better of her in some way. His sister was strong and she used to pinch him; long, methodical pinches during which she folded his flesh over and gave a twist, or she would dig her fingernails in. Karl bit his fingernails and, like his overeating, wished that he didn't. 'Look at your hands. they are disgusting,' his mother said, 'you have made yourself bleed. Why must you chew your fingernails. Look at your father's hands, they are beautiful. Once in a train a lady spoke to me and she said, "I know your husband is somebody important, I can tell by his hands." If you have nice hands you get on and people will think you care for yourself.' Karl agreed – and went on biting his nails. They gave him a clasp knife because they thought that not being able to open the clasp knife would encourage him to grow nails, but he found he could open the knife if he grew the nail of one finger.

The holiday home had been recommended by the other Hartlands and that was good enough. The children were met from the boat and Karl noticed a sign hanging from a telegraph pole which said JEWS NOT WANTED HERE. He wondered whether they should turn back, but his sister said, 'Take no notice.' That sort of sign was appearing all over the place. Father took some notice, though. He would always look first, then walk away if there was a sign which said that. 'If they don't want us,' he said, 'we won't spend our money there.'

The holiday home was run by 'aunties' and the children were put in dormitories according to age. Some afternoons his sister would take him out and buy cakes and ice cream and they talked. One day Karl had been slapped by one of the 'aunties' and his sister thought it wasn't fair, but he wasn't quite sure. She had told him to get washed and he had muttered 'stupid cow' and she had turned round and smacked him in the face.

There was another boy from Essen at the holiday home. His name was Alfred, and he was the son of one of Mutti's best friends.

Alfred was Karl's 'friend'. They had gone to the same elementary school but he had not got into a gymnasium, and Karl's mother said darkly that he needed extra lessons. The holiday together was not a great success as Alfred was a sneak: he reported Karl for stealing two bread rolls with sausage on them. All the rolls had been laid out ready for supper on plates in neat rows and Karl had gone in and taken two. Because Alfred was a sneak, Karl had been told off in public: 'You have taken someone else's food so you can do without. It's a good thing that your sister is here, we can tell from her that you come from a decent family,' the lady in charge of the home had said, and Karl hated her and seethed with ideas for revenge. The worst thing, though, was Alfred's treachery.

'Well, people are like that,' his sister said.

'But he was my friend.'

'Well he is a creep and we will all call him a creep.' The children who were on Karl's side did not speak to Alfred after that.

The best thing about the home was that he seemed to be appreciated, and was not always held to be in the wrong as at school. Also the home had a part of the beach reserved for its children and they played there and made huge castles. Some were decorated most carefully with wet sand and flags. A common ornament was the spread out eagle clutching a swastika in its claws and there were small red flags with the white circle and black swastika in them. People sunbathed in bathchairs that looked like halved peanuts. They were made of basketwork and if anyone was changing they would hang a towel over the upper half and would struggle into or out of their costumes behind the towel. Karl and his friends would draw each others attention to any grown-up they might see naked and they thought it hilarious when they glimpsed a breast or some pubic hair.

The great success of the holiday, however, was the black plastic mac. Karl would tighten the belt, and one of the aunties put him in charge of the little ones and he drilled them as if they were soldiers. They did drill in the playground at school and the teacher shouted, blew whistles and made them do about turns. Karl often got it wrong and would be bellowed at. His grandfather had told him that with peasant boys in the army they taught them about left and right by sticking straw in the right and hay into the left jackboot; then the sergeant would shout 'straw' instead of right turn because they understood that. Karl enjoyed shouting at the little ones and they seemed to like being shouted at. At least they didn't cry or go away, and so he led his little army into the pine forest and they made guns out of branches and shot at each other and fell about when dead, over and over again. 'Come on Lieutenant Hartland,' the auntie would say, 'you look very smart, like a real officer.' And he preened himself, imagining he was thin and muscular and in charge of a great army.

There were trips to other islands near to Wyck, which had huge yellow dunes and enormous beaches. When it was low tide the children were led from one island to the next and that was exciting. Many people had died, the aunt told them, because they got the tide times wrong; they would be halfway across the sand when the water rose. People on the shore heard the cries but no one could help, and later the bodies were washed up on the beach.

The children found many treasures on the beaches. Karl found a tropical helmet which still had a piece of silk ribbon on the side but it was too big to wear. For a time he walked with a girl called Ilse and they had sudden friendly fights and rolled all over each other and he liked being near her, but then some-one teased him, saying, 'You're keen on Ilse.' And he didn't want anyone to think that, so he didn't walk with her again.

Towards the end of the holiday the lady who ran the home called Karl and his sister into her room. 'I am afraid I have to tell you your grandmother has died,' she said. 'I am very sorry.'

Neither of the children said anything much. 'Why did she die?' asked Karl.

'She was old and ill and she died very peacefully. Your mother asked me to tell you that she died very peacefully,' she said, almost as an afterthought.

There was nothing more to be said and the children trooped out of the room. Karl felt bad. He thought he ought to cry because his grandmother had died, but he did not feel like crying because Grandma Freudenberg had never been very nice to him. At any rate that was how it had seemed to him. She was just an old fusspot who told him not to touch things and not to eat the things he liked; in fact if she had had her way she would never have let him out of bed. He remembered how once he had come home from the builder's yard with blood streaming down his face. He had hit his head against a nail on a wooden plank and it hadn't even hurt, but then he had felt something wet on his face and when he saw it was blood he began to run howling with fear rather than pain. Grandma Freudenberg was in charge that day, and she gave a shriek of panic which made Karl even worse. 'Blood, you naughty boy, how did it happen? Look out! You'll get blood on the good carpet. What shall I do? Sit down, I'll call Dr Levi. Hold this,' and she pressed a handkerchief into Karl's hand, and he held it to his head. Then the handkerchief got stuck to the clotting blood and by the time Dr Levi came it had started to bleed again.

Dr Levi had a long face, a goatee beard and his head was shaved all clean like Grandpa Freudenberg's. He was an old friend of the family, and was not slow to tell Grandma that it was a complete waste of time calling him and that she had made a fuss about nothing. Her daughter, he added, would not have made such a to do over a bit of blood, she had seen too much in her time. Karl's mother had been a nurse during the war so she knew many of the local doctors and they seemed to think very highly of her.

In the end Karl did cry a bit, and walked with his sister on the dyke, feeling for the first time possibly that they did not have to hate each other and fight for points of advantage.

'She was a great beauty in her time,' said Margot. 'Mutti told me that she could not bear to be old and she was only so awful to everyone because she hated losing her good looks. She came from a very strange family and most of them came to no good and wasted large fortunes. They are not a bit like the Hartlands who save everything.' Karl remembered the monthly savings ceremony and agreed.

When they got back to the home everyone was nice to them. Even the 'auntie' who had clipped Karl for calling her a cow said, 'Oh you poor boy, your granny has died, how sad.' Karl hoped he looked serious and tragic and somehow purified by the pain of the experience. The other children did not say very much to them but he felt important and that was precious to him.

When they arrived home the children were met at the station by their mother who was wearing black. The funeral had been the week before and she said she was glad the children had been away on holiday and had been saved from all the upheaval. 'Be nice to Grandpa Freudenberg,' she said, 'he is very lonely now.' Karl swore a solemn oath to himself always to be nice to Grandpa Freudenberg, not to frighten him or tease him. When the children went into the house their grandfather was waiting for them, and Karl asked if he felt like a game of chess. From then onwards they played chess together, and what Karl liked best was that he could win against his grandfather. His father had taught him to play but he would never let him win and Karl hated losing all the time. One day when they were playing his father had gone out of the room and Karl had quickly rearranged the pieces to his own advantage. When his father came back he quietly rearranged the pieces as they had been before and said nothing about it; Karl hated himself for being caught at cheating. Grandfather spent the evenings after supper in the renaissance drawing room, sitting by the huge desk and reading while the rest of the family were in the room above.

'We have entered you for some classes in physical training,' said his father before school began again. 'You must be better at physical training in school; that's the trouble with us, we have allowed ourselves to become too soft.'

So Karl began going to classes at Mr Charc's academy for physical fitness. Mr Charc told Karl he had been a local boxing champion in the Düsseldorf area. He was a short man, very fair, very jolly and full of bounce. He had huge shoulders and fine curly fair hair on his chest. He wore very short swim shorts and high lace up boxing boots. He lived in the house belonging to Grandfather Freudenberg's cousin, whom Karl called 'the budgerigar': his neck and the back of his head were all part of the same curve and his nose had the same curvature as the bird. Mr Charc had the whole ground floor and the drawing and dining rooms had been turned into a gymnasium of sorts. There was a leather couch where he used to do massage, hooks in the ceiling for a trapeze, hooks which had skipping ropes hanging from them and, in one corner, a vast selection of weight-lifting equipment. Boxing gloves of all sizes were hanging from hooks and there were bottles of various liniments on a shelf. Mr Charc always rubbed suntan oil into himself and the whole place smelt of it; it was a nice warm smell and Karl liked it. 'He likes Jews,' said Mutti, 'and he can get a good lot of custom from all you fat softies.'

Certainly Mr Charc profited from the need of the better off among the Jewish community to prepare themselves for the new national idea of lean toughness. Both children were entered for classes twice a week, and once a week Karl was on his own for half an hour. First he would be suspended by his arms from

43

the wooden bars and told to lift his legs up . . . 'Make your stomach strong.' Then he was hung from a rope attached on the ceiling . . . 'Make you grow.' And then there were endless sweaty exercises with small iron bars which he gripped in his hands. Mr Charc always did all the exercises with his class, but while Karl's iron bars were made from cast iron his were smooth stainless steel ones.

'Come on, boxing next,' he would shout, he himself dripping with sweat from all the work. 'Come on, boy, hit me.' Karl lunged forward and missed him. 'You are too slow, come on, footwork is everything. I only lost fights when my footwork wasn't right. Come on, come on!' Karl would close in, afraid to hit in case he would be hit back. Mr Charc weaved round and round him muttering and teasing, but he was never unkind and Karl loved his lessons. 'Come on, jiu jitsu.' Again wild lunges, grapples and falls. But among all the sweat Karl learnt grips, and his footwork got better. His parents were delighted and put a couple of metal handgrips in his bedroom and later a chest expander.

If the object of the exercise was to make Karl thinner it was not much of a success. After each strenuous session he would adjourn to an afternoon snack of beef tea made from greasy yellow cubes, ham rolls and rock cakes. Then he would buy sliced smoked beef, salami or ham from a butcher on the way home and in the dark he would wolf down the slices, finally throwing the paper away. He would then come home for the family supper.

Grandfather came to all the family meals and gradually Karl became aware that the old man was a noisy and messy eater. The others must have noticed it too but they loved him and accepted the failings of old age. But Karl could not make it out. All he knew was that he was constantly told off for such behaviour – for stuffing things into his mouth, making slurping noises, burping and not keeping his arms down while holding his knife and fork. 'When your mother went to the finishing school,' his father told him, 'they put books under her arms and when she dropped them she knew that she wasn't

44

eating properly.' His mother had more to say. 'We had to walk with books on our heads to teach us good posture, and we wore gloves all the time and we had to speak French like this, and she would break into an exaggerated French diatribe which had the children rolling on the floor with laughter.

The French had lived in Grandmother Hartland's house and in the Freudenberg house during the French occupation of the Ruhr. Karl had not been born when they were there, but his sister had learnt to speak French because the officers had brought their families with them. They had behaved like perfect gentlemen, his mother said, except for one unfortunate Belgian who had wet his bed when he came in in a drunken stupor. The French had given them food secretly and had shared what they had in the way of rations. Their experience was very different from the stories of horror Karl had been told in school, where the great hero was one Schlageter, who had been shot for attempting to sabotage a train carrying coal out of the Ruhr. Nevertheless, his father felt strongly about the disgrace of Versailles. 'We were treated very unfairly,' he said on one of their walks. 'All the nations ganged up on us; we were starving and the fight could not go on. Then they took everything away from Germany, our colonies, the Saar, everything.'

The walks were usually on Sundays, and Karl liked to walk with his father for the men's talk; his mother and Margot would follow behind. There were several walks and each one had a special aim: one was to a bridge to 'feed the fishes' which meant in fact, to spit down into the water. Then there was a walk by a huge reservoir that ended up with lemonade for Karl and brandy for his father. Sometimes they would talk Latin to each other. Latin was taught at the school and father was keen on the classics. 'Ubi sunt feminae, Carolus?' 'Feminae sunt in silva, pater.'

Father had a gift for telling stories. The ones Karl liked best were about his childhood – for example when he had broken his leg. It had happened, Father said, when they were playing in the cellar of the old house where the bank was and where Grandmother Hartland had lived. 'I stayed in hospital for weeks and my leg was in traction.' 'Did it hurt?' Only when my brother came along and played with the strings and then my leg would bob up and down.' Father also had the ability to talk with his mouth shut and, as Karl would tell his friends excitedly, 'He can make voices come out of the coal heap.' Voices also came out of eggs and from under the table. Father only did his tricks rarely and sparingly, and this made them even more exciting. He could make coins come out of noses and cigar ends disappear.

On Easter Day the family always went for a walk, and when the cock crowed it was the signal for the egg trick; wherever the children looked, under trees or under bushes, chocolate eggs would appear and would be collected in bags, and then, when the cock crowed again, the eggs were finished. Poor old Grandfather Freudenberg was so impressed with this piece of magic that he tried to do the same thing in the garden, but within minutes Karl was clinging to his pocket, shrieking with delight, and pulling the chocolate eggs out, and that was the end of that great illusion.

School started again and Karl had a new form master, one Kosh, who had lived in Latin America and had returned to the land of his fathers. His hair was jet black, and his cheekbones high, but he was a great patriot and talked about the victimisation of Germans in South America. He sold the boys a calendar which had an atrocity recorded on each page: 'Mr – chased by a mob and lynched in the streets of Bogota. His crime: being a German.' Karl read the calendar and was much moved by the accounts.

The moment he was back in school all the old horrors began. 'You back again, thought you had gone to Palestine.' 'Why don't all the Jews go to Palestine and waddle round in the Jordan. Take a dip in Jordan water, Hartland.' The first essay, of course, was on 'What I did in the holidays'. Karpf had been to Switzerland and foolishly wrote about it. 'Listen boys,' said the English master, 'Karpf has been to Switzerland. Of course we can't all go, we aren't rich enough and it takes a lot of foreign currency.'

Foreign currency had to be preserved at all costs, that was the message of the day and Jews, being 'internationalists' were accused of taking their fortunes out of the country, thus impoverishing the poor and honest Germans. Karpf and his family were now found guilty of just that crime. Karl was happy that he had stayed within German territory, and he wrote about the dykes and the sailing ship. About the only thing that earned him any praise at all was his composition. He had been given top marks for a piece on how his frog had caught a fly. Karl had been given a terrarium and although the family was cross with him for cutting turf out of the centre of the lawn to furnish the bottom, they were pleased about the essay. 'We are always reminded of our son when we walk in the garden,' said his father grimly, thinking of the dead vine leaves and now the brown patches in the middle of the lawn.

In class Karl felt he could be somebody by making people laugh. No use wearing his smart black plastic mac and being a lieutenant here. They were always sneering at his unmilitary bearing. 'Keep your head straight! Why do you always put your head to one side?' the PE man shouted at him. Mr Charc had taught Karl how to climb up ropes and wooden bars. 'All you have to do, boy, is to push with your feet, don't make your arms do all the work.' And miraculously Karl moved up the rope, up and up to the top. Only, when he could do it, no one took any notice and his next area for agony was the huge vaulting box with a leather top. 'Over the top, legs apart,' came the shout. Karl ran at it with all his might and ended up half across, sitting astride, not knowing how to get where he had wanted to be. The whole form laughed loud and long and he tried to join the laughter but he just blushed.

Every week Karl and Karpf spent a period together when the other boys had religious instruction; a Catholic priest came to see the Catholics and a pastor came to see the Protestants. The two Jewish boys spent the period in what had long ago been a school detention room, but detention was now done in ordinary

47

classrooms. It had an old desk in it and iron bars on the windows. Karl and Karpf niggled at each other for as long as they could bear to speak to each other at all. They had met socially once or twice at the other Hartland's house by the lake. Karl had then made common cause with Lutz, and once they enticed Karpf into the lift and then Lutz stopped it halfway between floors. The hapless Karpf was rescued by the English nanny who called them wicked boys in her funny, broken German, but she wasn't all that serious and the boys gathered that she didn't like Karpf either.

Later there were to be more 'free' periods because lessons were included to increase the boys' Germanic self-awareness and it was not thought right that Jews should attend these. There had been one embarassing incident in the geography class when the teacher had picked out Karl to demonstrate the Aryan type. 'You see,' he said, 'here we have the blond hair and blue eyes, and notice the head shape, not round like negroes but high at the back denoting intelligence.' The class listened in appalled silence. They did not have much time for Karl, on the other hand, no one liked the geography master and so they said nothing.

'Sit down, boy,' said the geography master. 'What's your name?'

'Hartland.'

'The banker Hartland?'

'Yes.'

'Oh my God, sit down.' It was a sweet moment for the whole class and in the playground they said to Karl: 'Made a fool of old Greif, stupid sod he is, good old Hartland.'

Karl was almost drunk with all the attention he received, it was just like one of the best day-dreams which he had in many lessons. There would be an edict from above that the Jews were to be re-admitted to favour. Their long and meritorious contribution to German history would be acknowledged and Karl saw himself on a triumphal waggon surrounded by cheering masses. Everyone waved little flags and cheered, people smiled at him when he came to school and everything was going to be lovely.

This sudden recognition made him feel he could become one of the boys, and so he decided to play funny tricks. He bought itching powder from a little stationery shop just behind his home. All their things for school were bought there – pencils, paper, glue, and there was one special room for textbook exchange. All the books you needed were written on a list at the beginning of the school year, and each year the old ones were taken to the shop and exchanged for new ones. In fact the old lady who ran it knew exactly what new books were needed and as the Hartlands were old customers she always had nice clean copies available. She never forgot to ask after the family and said that she was sorry Karl's grandmother had died.

The itching powder was sold in small red round cardboard boxes. In class Karl stuck some powder into the collar of the boy in front of him, and the boy wriggled and writhed as if he was having an epileptic fit. The master asked, 'What's up?'

'Someone has stuck itching powder down my neck.'

The teacher was the art teacher. He wore his white collar over his jacket and had no tie. This showed that he was an artist and not bound by ordinary social conventions. Karl actually liked to draw and paint and felt less hunted in the art room than elsewhere. Not that he got much encouragement. 'Where did you copy that from?' the art master said when Karl brought him a painting of a cowboy and an Indian. In a sense, it was a copy. The two figures were toys Karl had and he had put them on a book in front of him and had drawn them. To him copying was taking a drawing from another drawing and pretending it was your own, so he felt a burning sense of injustice and hated the art teacher.

'Who did it?' said the art teacher. 'Own up.'

Karl put his hand up hoping that such righteous honesty would be appreciated. 'Oh you,' he said, 'I might have known, I'll enter your name in the register.'

This was a serious matter; if a master entered a boy's name in the register the form master knew that there had been misbehaviour of some sort or other and he would deal with it

49

as he thought right. In the book, in beautifully flowing writing, it read: 'K. Hartland brought itching powder into the art class and put it down another boy's neck and created a disturbance. Signed – G. Shiedl, Art Master.'

Mr Kosh called Karl over after the break. 'What's this?'

Karl went very red and stuttered that he had indeed put itching powder down a boy's neck and that he was very sorry. 'For a boy in *your* situation it is very unwise to do anything that attracts special attention,' said Mr Kosh. 'You know there is a quota for your people and you are lucky to be here at all; now you make a nuisance of yourself. An hour's detention next Saturday.'

Karl heaved an inward sigh of relief. Saturday was all right. he was supposed to go to the youth service at the synagogue but that could easily be skipped and he did not have to tell his parents that he had got into trouble at school. He phoned up the secretary at the synagogue from home saying that Karl Hartland could not come on Saturday but that he would be there next week. On Saturday he went off to school. Everything was closed The main entrance, which looked like a Greek temple entrance, was shut and so he thought that no one was there. He stood in the yard and waited for someone to fetch him in or for something to happen. After what he thought was an hour, which he spent kicking the ice off puddles and inspecting the pig bin, he left.

On Monday Mr Kosh said, 'What happened to you? Why didn't you turn up for detention?'

'I was there,' said Karl. 'I was in the yard for an hour and no one came for me.'

'Why didn't you go to the detention room?'

'The front door was locked.'

'What about the back door?'

It had not occurred to Karl that there was another entrance into the school for an event as important as the detention session and no one had told him what to do.

'You had better come again next week,' said Mr Kosh, and made an entry in the book.

Karl felt outraged. It wasn't fair. He had come to the school and no one had told him what to do. A tiny flame of resentment and rebellion rose within him. He just wasn't going to turn up. Why should he? He had owned up and if that boy hadn't sneaked on him he wouldn't have been in trouble and he knew he could not phone the synagogue secretary a second time. He was lucky to have got away with it once.

So on the next Saturday he went to the youth service and his religious instruction at the synagogue. He went in by the side entrance. The service consisted mainly of bible stories which Karl liked, particularly when he was allowed to tell his own version of the story to the class. This was more like the old moments of glory when he had been put in front of the class in the elementary school.

The children were also taught Hebrew and by this time Karl could read the alphabet, but could not understand a word of what he read. Lutz, the other Hartland, also came to the service and the boys would wander off afterwards and would refresh themselves at the 'automatic restaurant'. This was a marvellous place which Karl felt made paradise unnecessary. A coin put into a slot would produce a flow of lemonade, coffee or whatever, and Karl remembered happily how once the tap just went on flowing and he had managed to fill several glasses of lemonade while it just went on running. After the 'drinks' you came to glass cases and in them were rolls and cakes. The rolls were decorated artistically: the salami rolled into delicious cones, resting on glistening potato salad, garnished with slices of pickled green cucumber. Or there was smoked salmon with a slice of egg on top and a few grains of black cod's roe on top of that.

Karl had to be careful to have enough money on him on these occasions and so paid particular attention to his father's money boxes beforehand. He had by now learned to leave the small coins and go firmly for the larger denominations. There was a change machine at the restaurant so he could put his money in and then share the handful of coins that came out with Lutz. Lutz was doubtful. He led a more sheltered life than Karl and had been severely warned about all food in public places. And ham was not allowed in his home. 'It isn't that we are religious,' he said, 'but Mother promised her mother that she would never touch ham and she never has.'

'You didn't promise?' asked Karl.

'No.'

'Well, in that case it's all right; you aren't breaking any rules.'

Karl uneasily remembered a joke about a Jew who went up to a counter and asked, 'How much might that ham be?' There was a clap of thunder. The old Jew looked upwards and said, 'Well, one may ask, may one not?'

So Lutz was bought his ham roll and Karl watched him, fascinated, wondering whether there would be a clap of thunder or what. Nothing happened except that Lutz enjoyed his ham and Karl felt that his faith was further diminished. He already had doubts on Friday evenings, when closing his eyes towards the candlelight produced fewer mystical thrills than it had done when he was smaller.

On Monday Mr Kosh asked him over and wanted to know why he hadn't turned up again. Karl could not say that he thought it was unfair and that he was never, ever going to turn up, so he muttered that he had been feeling sick. Mr Kosh became very cross. 'Stand to attention! Don't just mutter at me, boy! Come on, attention! Hands along the trouser seams! What do you think we are running here? You'd better make sure that you turn up this Saturday.'

Karl was in despair. Illness and a note from his mother was the only hope. But what illness. I'll feel sick and I'll stick my finger down my throat and that will do it. He found that making himself sick with a finger down his throat was easy, but he also knew that his parents were not very impressed with that trick. So on Friday evening he made a small wound in his leg with a knife.

'For God's sake the boy is bursting at the seams,' said his mother when she saw the cuts. 'How did you get them?'

'I cut myself and I feel sick.'

A thin bandage was applied to the leg and on Monday Karl

limped up to the form master. 'I injured my leg and I couldn't come on Saturday.'

'It's no use pretending you are ill, Hartland. You will come next Saturday and I am going to write to your father to make sure that you do.'

This was a disaster and Karl felt his campaign of defiance was threatened. The whole point had been to avoid letting the family know – and now this.

The mail always came early, so Karl hovered in the cloakroom at the side of the main entrance, and on Tuesday he spotted the school letter. It was in a blue envelope and had no stamp on it. He grabbed it quickly dashed into the guest lavatory and tore it open. It said: 'Your son's presence is requested at the detention session next Saturday. Would you please ensure that he is present and sign this letter below.' Karl decided that all he had to do was to sign the letter in writing like his father's and all would be well. He stuck the letter into his pocket and went to school feeling relieved that he had found a solution to his problem.

Before lunch that day his mother said, 'Go up to your father.' This was unusual and she looked serious. Karl's knees felt shaky as he went up to the living room where lunch was already set out on the table. His father looked serious. He had thick black eyebrows and they seemed thicker than usual. 'Where is my letter?' he asked. Karl meekly took it out of his pocket and handed it over.

'It is my letter and you took it. Do you realise that taking other people's letters is a serious crime?'

Karl knew it was because he knew the story about the special postmen who took money round. Someone had told him that if a money-carrying postman went wrong, he was never brought to trial, he just hanged himself. Karl muttered something about being sorry and the family sat down to lunch as if nothing had happened. Margot sensed the atmosphere and asked what was up.

'Your brother,' said Mutti, 'has been taking your father's mail, and he is in trouble at school.'

Margot never got into trouble at school. She did all her homework neatly and she was well liked and had very good reports, and she drew rather well. She just snorted and looked at Karl who went very red and went on trying to fish noodles out of his clear soup. The next Saturday he reported at the school and found the right room.

'Oh, there you are,' said the master in charge. 'We have been waiting for you for a long time. Sit down.' And so Karl sat down and read for an hour.

Chapter 4

Gerda, the Hartlands cook, had black hair and she was a devil in the kitchen, Karl's mother said. She never felt that she could go into the kitchen comfortably because Gerda scowled at her and would not tell her where things were. Mutti had learnt to cook at her finishing school but was not allowed to practise her skill except on Gerda's day off and she was far too good to the servants her 'friends' said. The servants often had the same food as the family, they had their own bathroom and they had a washbasin in their bedroom. Their sheets had once been red and white check in coarse cotton specially bought for them, but in time they were allowed white sheets. As all the linen came from the Freudenberg store, it was perhaps easier to be generous with linen. The maids were also given packs of linen as presents for Christmas.

The Hartland household had two celebrations at Christmas time. The first was the Jewish festival of Chanukah. Candles were lit, one more every morning for seven days to commemorate the heroic resistance in the temple during the revolt against the Romans, and special Chanukah songs were sung. Mutti never took these celebrations entirely seriously and got the giggles when either Father got the prayer wrong or the candles tipped over. Karl realised it was all done for the children, to give them a religious background, rather than for its own sake. Anyhow he liked Chanukah because it really was a substitute for Christmas and he was given presents. His parents were afraid of spoiling the children with too many presents but there were things like books, toy soldiers and plates of honeycake biscuits, nuts and oranges. The maids had a Christmas tree, but Karl knew it was only a side-benefit for him and it wasn't *his* Christmas. He had grumbled about it to Malli, who had taken him to a Catholic church to show him the figures portraying the nativity. They were huge figures and there was straw on the stable floor. A record player played 'Holy Night' and Karl was much moved. Much better than the Jewish Christmas, he told Malli, and she just smiled to herself. Although he had his presents at Chanukah, Karl felt curiously deprived when the maids had their Christmas. They gave him some small presents and he played with them furiously as if to show the world that he was not greedy. Karl remembered one Christmas when the maids were saying 'Thank you very much' for their piles of sheets and pillow cases and he had sat in the corner, playing with the one soldier he had been given. It was a standard bearer, wearing a half-moon shape silver plaque round its neck, and tactfully the flag was red, white and black and not one with a swastika. The maids put the sheets away. They were to help them with a trousseau when they got married.

Apart from the children's maids, who did not seem to stay long after Malli, the rest stayed a long time. It was said that Jews were good to work for, generous and not stringent in their demands. But this did not stop the drift. Gerda, Karl discovered, was a member of a National Socialist organisation for young women. One day Karl looked into the cupboard in her room and he saw the uniform hanging up. He told his mother about it and she was upset that Gerda was a member but she also didn't want to have to admit that Karl had been spying and did not quite know what to do. He did sometimes sneak into the girls' room; he did not quite know why. It was partly just boredom and partly to find out more about women. He looked at underclothes that were lying about, he opened drawers and sniffed the various bottles. He was puzzled by pieces of cotton with button loops at each end. He was even more intrigued when his question, what were they for, was received with shrieks of laughter. 'You are a one. I bet you are going to be a real menace when you get a bit older.' He saw these garments hanging on the washing line, and he had once seen one stained with spots of blood. He hoped to find love letters or letters home, but it was mainly the mystery of a room in which girls were sleeping that drew him to snooping around. Karl's own room was on the same floor as the maids and it was easy for him to know when to go in and have a look. There was a long corridor lined with huge wardrobes. These were full of sheets and table linen. Each piece of linen was embroidered with the initials of the family. The great wash was done only once every four weeks and so a big stock was needed. When the sheets were dirty they were put into wicker baskets in the cellar. They were soaked, and there was a huge washing machine and a spin dryer. Karl knew when it was wash day because the house smelt of soap, sheets, steam and boiled sausage. Extra help came, and when the things had been washed they went up to the ironing room and the ironing lady came for several days and worked on the sheets which then went back into the cupboards after airing.

The first room along the corridor was the ironing room. Margot once left the electric iron on and it burned through the boards of the ironing table and left a black smouldering hole. Father came up and smacked her face. Much as Karl disliked his sister he felt very frightened when she was smacked, and cried more than she did, but it was more from fear than sympathy. His father frightenened him at times even though he could be full of tricks and jokes. It was just his dark eyebrows. He never hit Karl, as his sister noticed with some bitterness.

Karl's room was next to the ironing room and at the end of the corridor were the maids' rooms and their bathroom and lavatory which Karl also used. When he wanted to tease the maids Karl put monsters at the end of the corridor. Once he had been too successful. He had built up a man, stuffing old trousers with rags, pinning a shirt to the wall and topping it with a carnival mask of a clown. The effect was enhanced by torch bulbs in the eyes which were connected to a battery. Over the whole creation he draped a light green diaphanous piece of veil. The veil had belonged to one of his mother's fancy-dress costumes and Karl had found it in a box full of oddments. As the maid came up the stairs Karl was waiting behind his half-open door. Instead of bursting into laughter and congratulating him on his clever creation she began to scream and scream and wouldn't stop. The others rushed up the stairs. Karl hastily closed the door and crept under his bed. He heard comings and goings, the screaming stopped and was replaced by hiccup-like sounds and muttering. The maid did not stay long after that. Mutti was furious with him and said, 'Stand in the corner.' And he stood there, feeling sorry for himself but hating being out of his mother's favour, and so he tried to punish himself by digging his remaining finger nail into his hand, hoping that it would bleed and that everybody would be sorry for him.

New laws came out: no Jewish household was allowed to have non-Jewish servants under its roof. The idea was to protect the racial purity of the German maids and to make sure that they were no longer ravished by Jewish fathers or sons. Gerda and the maid left, full of tears and carrying wicker baskets with their things in them. New ones had to be found, and Father and Mutti became gloomy about the prospect of Jewish maids. When the family were on their own they referred to the maids as 'the ladies' or sometimes as 'schicksen'. That was a Yiddish word and was meant to be rude and contemptuous. 'Don't you ever dare say that to the girls,' said Mutti, 'it is very rude and nasty and we don't really use words like that except when we are among ourselves.' This was said with such emphasis that Karl never, even in his greatest anger, used the word. There were other Yiddish words that were not to be used, or only when the family was together and no outsider present. Anything that resembled Jewish or Yiddish culture had more or less been eliminated from speech and custom. It went pretty far – garlic was particularly associated with Polish Jews and was therefore not used in the house; hair had to be short – no one wore the long sideburns of the orthodox. The Yiddish word 'meschugge', meaning 'mad' was used as a mild term of abuse but with caution; Karl would call his sister 'meschugge' but no one else.

The Jewish maids were recruited through the office of the

Jewish Community, and before long two of them arrived, accompanied by their mother and father, who wanted to see that all was in order for their daughters. They inspected the beds, the washbasin and the bathroom, and wanted to know about the food and conditions of work. Mutti was clearly irritated by such questioning: it was one thing to be liberal and generous by choice and quite another to be expected to be all this as of right. Later when the family was together in the living room, she told them how cross she had felt.

One of the sisters, Ella, had bright red hair, was small, rather fat and had a habit of letting her hand droop limply downwards while she held her arm up. She looked fierce, Karl thought, and he moved with some care when she was about. He didn't pull at her apron strings for quite some time.

Ella's sister seemed completely overwhelmed by the move, and looked frightened and homesick. Her name was Eve, and Karl decided that it would be easier and less dangerous to tease her. Whenever he played Eve up, Ella seemed to be pleased, and before long it appeared that the two were not on good terms.

At about this time Karl had taken a dislike to washing. Grownups were always chasing him about his dirty neck, his knees and his hands. It was a battle of cunning that he tended to lose, specially while there was a maid looking after him, but now that the house was in the care of Eve and Ella Karl did rather better. First there was the matter of underpants: he did not like his school very much, and even less physical training, but he loved his PT pants. They were carmine red with blue stripes running down the sides and he much preferred them to the usual underpants, and so he wore them instead, week after week. If anyone spotted them he would say, 'I am wearing them because it is PT today,' or 'I am going to my lesson with Mr Charc later.' The trousers lost their bright colour and there were black rims on the pieces which rubbed against the top of his legs, but Karl watched the patina develop and it was weeks before his sister destroyed what might have been a mighty record by shrilly telling their mother, 'The dirty little beast hasn't taken his pants off for weeks and he smells.' Karl felt happy and contented when he added up and found he had worn his gym pants for seven weeks.

His parents sighed over the sisters. Somehow their Jewishness added to the complexity of the relationship between master and servant. Here were further obligations, burdens and responsibilities far beyond anything they had experienced before. Ella was no respecter of persons and would address people with the familiar 'thou' rather than the polite and more formal 'you'. She would stand in the door, leaning against the lintel, one arm against her waist, the other hanging down limply, her hand dangling as if attached to the arm by a thin string. 'What is it you want now?' she would ask, or grumble, 'Wait. I'll do it when I am ready.'

Mutti was always watching the girls. 'Tell me if you see them pinch anything,' she said to Karl, who thought this was an odd order after the telling off he had had when he had reported Gerda's uniform. But he enjoyed his detective duties and in due course found some embroidered flowers on Eve's night table which had come free in his father's cigarette packets. Full of eagerness to demonstrate his own honesty and integrity he reported this to Mutti. She seemed sad and not very grateful. 'And she eats like a horse,' she said. Not that anyone in the family or anyone else for that matter was grudged food, but Eve's appetite was enormous and she grew fatter visibly, stuffing bread, sausage, or, as an in-between snack, the veal that had been intended for supper. 'She will have to go,' said Mutti after some weeks, and she discussed the problem with Ella who agreed. So the parents arrived and the wicker basket was trundled down the stairs. 'Little Eve', as Karl called her was weeping, and Karl felt guilty and knew that he was partly to blame. The sister bloomed after Eve's departure, however, and became nicer to Karl who was able to tease her. She gave him food whenever he appeared in the kitchen. 'Young men always like it in the kitchen,' she said and roared with laughter. She had a boy friend who was the son of the gardener. Karl liked him because he let him have rides on his bicycle. He rode it round and round the garden, tumbling into the rose bed and making deep marks in the gravel when he braked too sharply, but he learnt to ride the bike. The family would not allow him a bike of his own. 'It's too dangerous,' they said. But they let Karl use the gardener's bike.

Although he had learnt to shin up the pole and the rope, life did not become any happier in school. Once he had mastered the skill of climbing up the rope the iron bar became the place of horror and persecution. The metal gripped into Karl's legs and pinched him, he used to hang helplessly, unable to pull himself over the top while some of his classmates swung gracefully up with a full swing, jumped over the top of the bar and ended up on the thick canvas mat. He hung on to the bar for dear life, one leg over, the other dangling. There were giggles from the rest of the 'team'. 'Look at Hartland, he is stuck.' 'Come on, Hartland, you are not trying, what's the matter – too much ham for breakfast?' Karl despaired. It was no use. Once he just let go and fell on to the mat with a heavy thump. The fall knocked his breath out of him and he could only breathe in very shallow gasps. The PT man stood over him. 'Come on, get up, don't fake tiredness.' But Karl couldn't and in the end he was helped into the dressing room. 'You have had a knock,' said the PT man, 'better go home and rest.' Karl got dressed; breathing still hurt, and he made sure that no one could possibly tell that he was really better. So he went home, walking slowly, catching his breath and standing still, as if to advertise to the world at large that an injured hero was returning from the battlefield.

Ella let him in. 'What's up, have they thrown you out?' Karl thought a dramatic gesture was indicated so he staggered forward and let himself sink to the floor. 'God, he's fainted,' cried Ella and called for Mutti who saw her son collapsed. Dr Levi was called, diagnosed a cracked rib, and an elastic bandage was wrapped round Karl. When asked what was the matter with him, he would reply nonchalantly, 'Just a cracked rib, fell down during PT.' As the only pain, really, was from the discomfort of the bandage, Karl was able to appear heroic. Whenever anyone touched him he gasped with pain.

He was learning that absence from school was sweet and rewarding as everyone fussed at home and showed a good deal of sympathy. He became better at faking illness. It was easiest to announce in school that one was ill, and then to come home saying that one had been ill at school. The attacks could range from headache to puking. One embarrassing moment came at home when Karl put the thermometer against the hot bulb of the bedside lamp and the mercury shot up to the very top. Karl knew that just a few strokes above 'normal' was what really impressed. He tried to push the mercury column down but it stayed up stubbornly and in the end he panicked when Mutti came into the room and he broke the thermometer. Mutti knew enough about illness to be a bit sceptical always, and she took Karl's temperature up his rectum. First she put vaseline on the thermometer and then up it went. Karl hoped to put the temperature up by straining, but his mother said, 'Watch out, or it will break inside and you won't like that!'

Karl had a new problem at school, the German teacher, Mr Bartholomeus. He wore a brown suit with very thin red stripes and had the little badge in his lapel that Karl came to dread. It was the size of a small button and had first a black then a red and then a white ring and in the middle was a black swastika. Teachers who wore that button always seemed to go out of their way to say something unpleasant to Karl, either when they saw him alone or, much worse, in front of the whole class. Mr Bartholomeus made his position very clear when he came into the classroom on the first day of term.

'What a noise, what a noise, one might almost think this was a Jew school.'

The boys quietened down. He must have known who Karl was because he looked at him, raised an eyebrow and smiled ever so slightly.

A look of pure hate came from Brett, the brightest boy in the class. He had taken to wearing his Hitler Youth movement uniform in class. Karl was deeply envious. There was not only the brown shirt, the black trousers, black neckerchief and armband with the lightning rune on it, but a dagger. A dagger, a real dagger which he pulled out in front of a group of admirers. Karl stood at the back of the group, peering. The dagger was short, set in a black hilt and had Blood and Honour engraved on the blade. Brett saw Karl and waved the knife at him. 'This is not for dirty Jews,' he said, 'this is for real enemies.'

On Saturdays, the Hitler Youth went out for military exercises. 'It was hand grenades,' they said one Monday. 'Only wooden ones but you have to know how to throw them.' Karl invented military exploits which he told to his friend with the stick on the way home. 'We went on that exercise,' he would say, 'and I was leading the group, just reconnaissance, you know, but it was real practice. We were fighting the railway police.'

About a quarter of a mile from Karl's house there was a railway embankment and some railway police had been on a military exercise not long before, defending the railway. Karl had followed them at a distance and so he felt his story had a sufficient basis of truth to be acceptable.

He often told stories that he just made up on the spur of the moment. People who liked him, like his grandfather or Rudolf, just said 'Oh yes' and listened. Others said it was all lies and then Karl became anxious and tried to assure them that it was true and that he could prove it. Or he would say, 'I bet you it's true. What do you want to bet?'

There had been a bad moment after the holidays. He had impressed two girls at the holiday home with his account of his Alsatian dog, Hasso. He had not got a dog, of course, although he wanted one badly. Then one day the front doorbell rang and there were the two little sisters. One said, 'We have come all the way from Wuppertal to see the dog.' Karl, blushing deeply, said, 'Well you can't, he has been taken out for a walk.' They seemed very disappointed and walked away, back to their parents' car that was waiting outside.

At school Karl had read a story about an Alsatian called Tchambuli. Mr Bartholomeus had given them a booklet with the story in it. The owner, a forester, had this dog given to him and trained him to be obedient: he took the dog by the collar, then twisted it round until he was nearly throttled and threw him on his back. The dog felt that he had found his master and after that was always obedient and loyal to the death. He helped his

63

master in the fight against poachers, but in the end they were both shot. Even though he was bleeding to death the dog made his way back to his master and they were joined in death. Mr Bartholomeus thought the story illustrated the importance of obedience, loyalty and service. What Karl liked was just the thought of owning a dog. He talked to his father endlessly about dogs and how valuable they were to protect property, but the hint was not taken up.

Homework was a greater worry now that he was at the gymnasium than it had been. Karl had inherited a wooden desk with a lid and space for books inside. Margot had used it, but now she had finished with her secondary school and gone on to learn about commerce.

Karl sat at the desk but never for long; it was too much like school and he felt imprisoned in it. On the other hand while he sat there the family assumed he was working and he was treated with respectful consideration. His mother would even ask if he wanted something to keep him going. When he was interested he could do the work quite quickly. The compositions were easy enough but the mathematics was difficult for him. His father had decided he needed help with mathematics and he and Grandfather Freudenberg used to fire questions at him. 'What is ten per cent of twenty nine thousand marks?' 'What would be the compound interest, at five per cent on a thousand marks left in the bank for seven years?' Grandfather would add that if he wanted to be a banker like his father he had better get on with it. Karl was not sure that he did want to be a banker 'like his father'. Everyone asked him the question and he got bored with always saying 'yes' all the time, so he changed his answer and said, 'When I grow up I want to be a writer!' To which everyone replied, 'You will have to do a lot of composition writing in that case.'

His Latin homework often consisted of learning verbs and conjugations, and his father tried to help by testing whether he had in fact done his work. 'Come on, Karl, let's hear the declension of *lupus*.'

Karl just could not get it into his head.

'Come on, it's easy: *lupus, lupi, lupo, lupum*. Say it after me.'

Karl got it wrong again. At that point his sister entered the fray. 'Come on, I can say it. *Lupus, lupi, lupo, lupum*, I don't know any Latin and I have only just heard it. You are stupid.' Karl took a breath and tried again. The grammar book was lying on his father's knees on a cushion. That was the way his father always read books. He got it wrong again and both father and sister shouted 'no' and repeated the declension. Everything was swimming and he began to cry.

'Come on, once more and then we'll leave you alone.'

'Leave him be,' pleaded his mother, 'you are making him quite meschugge.'

Karl got it wrong again and rushed out of the room crying with shame and embarrassment, hating to be called stupid and hating himself for not being able to do a simple declension. But he knew it in class the next day and was given a good mark.

The Latin teacher was, as Joseph had predicted, the dreaded Ivan the Terrible. His head was shaved and he had a double roll of flesh at the bottom of his head, above his collar. He wore dark glasses and spoke sharply and precisely. 'He gives you a five as soon as look at you,' the boys said of him.

Another intriguing aspect of Ivan was the scar on his face. The scar was parallel with his nostrils and stretched right across his face. It was deep, more like a slit, because the skin above and below bulged over the actual cut and when his face moved the scar seemed to stay still.

'He must have got it as a student,' his father explained to Karl. 'He must have belonged to a duelling fraternity. Jews have never been allowed to join them, they are very anti-semitic. Your Uncle Arnold tried to get into one but it was no good. The members walk along the street in a university town and they insult each other, and the one who has been insulted must demand satisfaction and then they fight a duel. They make sure that no one is seriously injured by covering the really vulnerable places.

Karl wanted to know what the really vulnerable points were and he wondered if a doctor could cut one so that it would look as if there had been a duel.

'One could do that, but the real test of courage is to fight the duel.'

Father had not been to a university and he seemed very impressed with the duelling and the cutting up of faces. Several of the teachers in the gymnasium had scars like that but Ivan's was the best.

When he had not done his homework Karl learnt that all he had to do was to stutter during the beginning of the answer and then he would be told to sit down and just given a bad mark. He was no longer quite so terrified of getting bad marks. In the first place at home they seemed to believe him if he said he was doing quite well and had got a 'two', and secondly when he tried he was given reasonable enough marks to keep up the average. At least that's what he thought.

One morning a blue letter came through the letter box again. Karl had not been expecting trouble from the school after the detention row and he was very startled. Blue letters could only mean trouble, so he thought it best to pocket it to see what it was about. It was early in the morning when he found it and no one was about so he went into the kitchen and held the letter over the steaming kettle. 'I'll see what it is and then I will glue it up again,' he said to himself. The letter opened quite easily, he quickly put the kettle back and withdrew into the 'winter garden'. This was an open room with huge windows, full of plants and palm trees. The window could be opened wide, and in summer or early spring the family would sit there almost as if in the open. When it was really hot they went out to the veranda, but the winter garden was a quiet place, especially in the morning. Mutti would garden in it, putting on gloves and delicately digging among the pots with a miniature chrome spade. There was also a special watering can.

The letter said that Karl Hartland's performance in geography and mathematics was below standard, that he had to improve his standards or there might be the possibility of his having to repeat the year. Repeating the year – 'remaining stuck to the same bench' – the boys said. Karl feared that more than anything, disgrace to the whole family would follow, he was certain. As Mr

Kosh had said, 'A boy in your situation cannot afford things like that.' The dreaded *consilium abeundi* (the advice to leave) would surely follow.

The parent or guardian was asked if he would kindly sign the letter and return it to the school. Karl decided that he would sign the letter himself and send it back. The only reason why things had gone wrong last time was because his father had guessed there was a letter, or possibly one of the maids had told him that there was another letter and it was in a blue envelope.

In the meantime Karl had to practise writing his father's signature. His father held his pen between the middle fingers and so Karl thought if he did the same the signature would also look the same. He tried on rough paper and then he went on to the official letter. Immediately he lost his confidence and made a blot and ink went all over the place. It looked dreadful and not a bit like a grown-up signature. Karl was not entirely discouraged, though. He made a special excursion to his father's money box for money to buy ink eradicator, which came in two tiny bottles, one with blue stuff and one with white. It smelled of chemicals. Karl put on the first lot from bottle one. The ink dissolved into a small blue lake. He blotted it up and put on the stuff from bottle two. It said on the label: 'This will restore the whiteness of the paper and leave no trace of ink.' Possibly it might have done all that if Karl had not been in so much of a hurry, but as he tried to blot up the mess a hole appeared in the paper. He was in despair, and put the messed up paper into his pocket.

Before lunch his father again demanded to see the letter from the school. Karl felt quite paralysed and could hardly move; his breath would not come out properly. He could see clearly now: it was all hopeless. But he did not know how to explain how difficult things were for him at school and how he had done it all to preserve his father's good opinion.

His father looked at the letter and said: 'Now you are taking to forging, as well as misappropriation of mail.'

Karl said to himself, 'It's a good job he doesn't know about the money I have been taking.'

'What are we to do?' said Father. 'I just don't know.'

Karl was unable to say anything. He wanted to say that he was sorry, that he would work ever so hard, but nothing could come out. He wished his father would punish him and that he was not quite so upset. Karl decided to punish himself and went up to his room without lunch. He would stop eating altogether he decided, and then they would forgive him because they did not want him to starve. There was a brushing noise against the door and Ella came in with a tray. 'They have sent this up for you; I don't know why I should have to carry it up all these stairs.'

There was goulash and noodles, Karl's favourite dinner, and he ate it very happily, deciding that he would leave half because he had been so bad – and then suddenly the plate was empty.

In the evening his mother came into the bathroom and sat on the stool with the cork top that stood by the bath. 'You must understand,' she said, 'that your father is a banker. People must trust bankers, they must be completely reliable. He is worried because forging signatures is a crime and it really is serious. Why do you do it? You really shouldn't do it, after all we are respectable people. Do you know,' she went on, 'when you father was young he once went into a casino at Monte Carlo, and when his father got to hear of it he said, "What if any client of the bank should see you? Do you think he would leave his money with a man who went and gambled?" That's the sort of standard your father has to set himself.' Karl felt miserable and did not know what to say to that so he just sat there.

His parents took Karl with them for a short holiday at Easter. Margot was away and he enjoyed having both his parents all to himself. They stayed at a hotel in the Black Forest. His parents had checked beforehand whether Jews were 'unwanted' but apparently all was well. In the evenings Karl was looked after by a friendly room maid who told him that she had once waited on Lilian Harvey, the famous film star. Karl had seen her in a film and had liked her and was very impressed that anyone had known a great film star. The maid said, 'And do you know she was like everyone else. Very nice but just ordinary without making a fuss as artists so often do.' This was disappointing.

Karl had hoped that a star would be special and would not be like everyone else.

He loved going to the cinema and now that he was a bit older his parents allowed him to go on his own. The fleapit was only a short way from the house, just over the railway bridge and by the town hall. The main attraction was the number of films they showed. First a Western – Karl remembered the waggons forming a circle and the Indians charging round and arrows piercing the poor settlers. He had Indian and cowboy toy soldiers and he played that game for a long time. Newsreels came next – these had become full of National Socialist propaganda. There were pictures of Hitler smiling and shaking hands, Goering smiling and shaking hands, and battleships being launched. After the newsreel, a cartoon or a comedy, and Karl had tears streaming down his face, he laughed so much. The one he liked best was about a man and his wife; the man took the sausages and measured them against each other and gave the wife the smaller one, and then he caught his hand in a drawer. When Karl got home after seeing this film he felt elated, but his parents were cross because they thought he had sat through two continuous shows. Karl tried to tell them about the sausages but somehow no one was amused.

In the hotel he spent an afternoon playing with a small fountain, plugging up the spout for a while and then letting the water come out with some force and spout high up into the air. Before they left the hotel Karl plugged up the fountain. On the train home it suddenly occurred to him that the pipe might burst and then they would hold him responsible. He was afraid of getting into more trouble and he could see the headline in the *Stürmer* – JEW SABOTAGES GERMAN WATER SUPPLY. He was nervous of that paper and with good reason. Every morning on his way to school he saw the headlines on the wall newspaper. It was in a red case with a glass front and he often looked at it when he was sure no one was watching. It was full of cartoons of fat men with huge hooked noses and enormous bellies slavering over evenly featured but terrified girls. Words like 'international communist' and 'capitalist' appeared very often. There were suggestions of ritual murder and secret rites. Karl, who knew it bore no relationship to what he knew of Judaism read it with mild interest, mainly because he hoped that it might tell him more of the mysteries of sex, about which no one seemed prepared to come clean. One morning he was horrified to see the name Hartland in the headline, and underneath was a story all about this man who had ravished Aryan girls, and his name was Hartland. He just prayed that Brett and the others at school had not seen the paper. The headline was huge and it was printed in large Gothic print. That day nothing was said at school, and at home, when he mentioned the problem to Margot, she said airily, 'Oh that's the Munster branch.'

Margot was at home less and less, she lived her own life, and now that she had left her secondary school she seemed more remote and less threatening. Karl did not mention the paper to his father because he thought it would upset him; and if his father had seen it he did not discuss it with Karl, presumably so as not to upset the boy.

The next Monday comments were made in school: 'See the *Stürmer*, Hartland?' Brett asked. 'I see you are in it.'

'Not me,' said Karl, 'just the name.'

'You Yids are all the same, degenerate lot.'

Karl got ready to fight Brett. 'If you say that again, I'll fight you.'

The other boys were circling round, droning, 'Fight. Fight! Come and see the fight. The Yid is going to get bashed up.'

Karl did not care any more, and Mr Charc's lessons had given him some confidence. He thought that he would get Brett on the nose quickly and that might stop him. Brett was no fool. He somehow realised that although Karl was no good at PT he was not all that weak, and he did not want to get into trouble with the authorities either, so he decided to call it off and walked away muttering that he was not going to contaminate the honour of the Hitler Youth by fighting Jews.

The fight, or rather Karl's willingness to have one, eased relations with his classmates. They tended to ignore him rather than attack him. One day the form master said, 'Karpf has left.'

There was muttering round the room and some happy grins. This was news to Karl, and he heard later that the Karpf family had left the country. Karl was not surprised that Karpf had not said goodbye, and he experienced a sense of relief; at the same time he felt even more isolated.

'Why don't *you* go away?' asked Backe, who was smaller than Brett but also wore the insignia of the movement. 'This isn't your country, you don't belong her, get out.'

Karl wanted to remind him of the local history lesson when anyone in the class both of whose parents came from Essen had to put up his hand. Nearly everyone's hand went up. Then it came to grandparents, and Karl was among the few whose father's parents at least had been born in Essen. This was also true of his great-grandfather.

In the history classes the French were the hereditary enemy and all the lessons were about the wars against the enemies of Germany. There were no history textbooks. They had all been withdrawn and until new National Socialist versions came out there was nothing but the teacher, who dictated notes and gave inspiring addresses. He was another one with a scar on his face, not as huge as Ivan's, but he was younger and a reserve officer in the army. Once he had been away for manoeuvres and he told the boys all about it. 'We have got marvellous tanks now, fantastic; and good guns to use against French tanks.' The boys were all enthralled when he drew battle plans on the blackboard and described how the tanks moved and what it was like to drive one. 'Tell you what,' he said, 'I'll take you all to my barracks. Maybe we can get lunch there as well. In the army they serve food out of mobile canteens; pea soup, sausage and lots of it.'

Soon after that he said it was all fixed up and would they all bring one mark for expenses. They filed past his desk and put their money into a box. He looked up. 'You, Hartland, you are a Jew. Jews can't come into army barracks. Sorry, you will have to take your money back.' Karl got out of his desk and walked up to the front. He was given his mark and sat down again. Brett grinned at him and hissed, 'You would sell our secrets to the enemy.'

Karl was burning with shame. He wanted to revenge himself and did not know how to.

At home Grandfather Freudenberg asked, 'Is there much "risches" (anti-semitism) in the school?' and Karl said there wasn't and Grandfather said, 'Good, because it isn't very nice. I expect they leave you alone because you are so strong.' Karl felt he could not say anything. This was his problem and he had to deal with it in his own way. He felt that the answer might lie in magic. In his religious instruction lessons on Saturdays he had been told about the 'unmentionable' word, God. Jews were not supposed to use the word God at all. There were all sorts of other words but the actual word was too sacred to use. Karl imagined that he, too, knew a magic word and that it would bring revenge and destruction on all his enemies. He just *knew* the magic word, and he knew that all he had to do was to touch something three times, mutter the magic word and then the stone, or whatever he had touched would, one day, blow apart with a mighty bang. So Karl touched his desk and muttered the word. He touched the *Stürmer* wall newspaper, he walked along and touched more and more places. The end would come and it would be his doing. No one, but no one, was to know the word, it was dangerous and it would not work if he told anyone so he touched and muttered and he hoped.

Karl had an invitation. His Aunt Flora wanted him to visit her and her husband Julius at Aix-la-Chapelle. She was Grandfather Freudenberg's youngest sister. She was a child of a second marriage and therefore much younger than Grandfather. Karl had always liked her very much. She was direct and never talked down to him or made little jokes, and she listened to what he had to say.

Father said, 'They ought to have called her *Uncle* Flora!' She was in charge of the cloth selling business although officially it belonged to Uncle Julius.

Julius had one eye in which the brown and the black were all mixed up together and he was blind in that eye. 'Stuck a needle into it when I was an apprentice,' he told Karl. He loved cloth and whenever he saw some he would rub it between thumb and forefinger and would say, 'That's a nice bit of cloth. English?' He had a very special reverence for English cloth and would talk nostalgically about that country. It seemed a mysterious country to Karl. 'It was foggy,' Julius said. 'Once, in a proper pea soup fog, I couldn't find my way back to my own room and I had only been out to post a letter.' There was also the food. He said that they had soups that made your eyes water, they were so peppery, and there was 'curry'. It was made with rice and sounded very strange.

Julius probably did not like the Hartlands very much because he made jokes about them and how rich they were. 'I bet you all wipe yourselves on ten mark notes,' he teased Karl, who liked to be teased by Julius. 'No, with us it's hundred mark notes,' he would reply.

Julius and Flora lived in a terraced house. The cloth store was on the first floor and they lived above the store. Karl walked among the bales and was introduced to the storeman and the clerk. He liked the food they ate. It was hearty and very starchy. Huge chunks of boiled sausage in thick lentil soup which also had potato in it. It was all cooked together in a pressure cooker. Another good dish was apples and potatoes stewed together, served with liver fried in butter until the butter was almost black and the onions in it had turned dark brown.

Julius had very little time for religion. 'We had a boy once,' he said, 'he was a beautiful boy and he was clever. I was sure he was going to take over the business. "You are going to come into the firm," I said to him, when he was lying in his cradle. "You'll come into the firm." And then he was ill and I called the doctor and he said it was just a stomach ache and the next thing we knew was that he had peritonitis and within two days he was dead. And I went to the rabbi and he told me that it was all God's will, and I said to the rabbi, "How can it be God's will that a good little boy who never did anyone any harm should die just like that. If God is so cruel I don't want anything to do with him any more!"'

'And do you know,' added Aunt Flora, 'he meant it, he has

never been near a synagogue since that time and he has never given them a penny either.'

Flora also told him about his mother when she was a young girl. 'Your grandmother had great ideas and so they sent her to a finishing school in Brussels. She hated it there. I remember fetching her for an outing and as she came out to us she threw her gloves into the air and would not wear her hat while she was with us!' It was a good thing, Flora thought, that the war had given her a chance to get away from home for a bit or else she would have been completely spoiled. Her mother would not allow her to become a nurse at first but Grandfather Freudenberg insisted. If that had not happened she would have been a social butterfly and nothing else. They used to give magnificent parties, and once they all dressed up in Persian costumes and they borrowed lots of carpets from the store and all the rooms were hung with carpets. Karl knew all that, but it was good to be talked to and to hear about his mother when she had been young and to be taken into the confidence of a grown-up.

Chapter 5

Karl had a terrible stomach ache. He was writhing with pain and he felt sick. He was worried because his parents had gone away on a holiday to Switzerland. His father had fallen down and broken his arm and had had it in a splint for weeks. It was frightening to Karl to see people on whom he depended so completely being hurt and vulnerable. Father had fallen over, running for a tram, and Mutti said it had been a complicated fracture. Now he was well again they had gone away. Karl was cross that they could bear to be without him, but they said Margot would look after him and so would Grandfather Freudenberg. He felt unenthusiastic about that. Grandfather was getting older and since his wife's death he had let himself go. He no longer looked as if he had been 'peeled out of an egg'. His hair grew longer, sometimes more than a centimetre, and Karl would say to him, 'It's time the flies' legs were cut off, Grandpa.' 'Oh, is it,' he would answer, brushing his hand over his head. Hair was cut by Mr Hüser who came to the house once a fortnight. Father was first, then came Grandfather and Karl last. Karl hated that because the towel that was put around him had all the little hairs in it from the other two and they stuck into his skin. Father said, 'Well it's cleaner than going into a barber's shop; you can get all sorts of infections there and Mr Hüser has been coming here for ages.'

Grandfather also ate his food more and more noisily. It was worst on Sundays when the family met together for a particularly grand breakfast and there was a plate of ham and sausages. The liver sausage came in a plastic skin, all shiny and greasy; in fact there were two sorts of liver sausage: the rough one which had bits of fat and meat in it, and the smooth one which was easier to spread on bread rolls, and Karl preferred it. Grandfather Freudenberg would mash together pieces of matzo. This was supposed to be eaten only for Passover, but he liked it so much he kept a supply of it all through the year. He broke up the pieces and then put coffee and milk over it and sugar and then he slobbered it down. Karl hated him while he ate that foul mash. There he goes again the old slobberer he would say to himself, slobber slobber all over the place, the old fool, look how the liquid runs out of his mouth. Grandfather ate very quickly; Karl was always told off if he swallowed his food too fast.

'Just like Grandfather Freudenberg,' Mutti would say. 'Eat slowly, child, chew each bite twenty times and it will be much better for you.'

Karl just could not do that. He always ate as if famine was round the corner, but he did begin to hate his grandfather. Because he was getting old, his excursions to the lavatory became messy. The maids also made jokes about him and they watched him on his morning excursion to the loo. For this, although it was next door to his room, the one that had been Karl's, he always wore a little flat cap. In one hand he carried a newspaper and in the other a soft little rag. Grandpa's little bog rag, Karl called it. He never went into that lavatory if he could help it, and if he did he piddled all over the place so that Grandfather would get the blame. Karl found that he was not a bit afraid of him. Once Grandfather Freudenberg asked him to get a newspaper for him and Karl said, 'You are an old arsehole and I am not doing anything for you.'

'For God's sake, boy, don't say things like that. It is terrible to swear like that.'

'You are an old dog's pisshole and a shitty arse,' Karl said.

'Where did you learn language like that? You are supposed to come from a good family and you must not use words like that.'

The phrase 'dog's pisshole' Karl had in fact picked up from

76

his historical reading. Frederick the Great had said to his soldiers as they were storming the church at Leuthen and were beginning to fall back: 'Dogs' pissholes! Do you want to live for ever?' As for arseholes, that had come from his sister who had said to him, 'If you call people arseholes they get ever so cross.' And she seemed to be right.

'Look Karl, you are growing up and you will have to earn people's good opinion, and I can tell you that if you use language like that they won't want to know you.'

'Kiss my arse,' said Karl. This was another quotation from literature. *Götz von Berlichingen*, an early play by Goethe had that line in it and they read it in school; in fact the crucial line – 'tell the Emperor he can kiss my arse (slams the window shut)' was left in dots and the teacher, looking sly and wicked, had told the boys what it really was. Karl was delighted with this gem of information. He would say 'Götz' to his sister, put his tongue out and slurp it upwards in a very suggestive manner, and she would complain to her father that he was being rude. Sometimes, though, she would giggle and do it back at him.

Karl felt curiously elated; this was the first time in his life that he had completely defied an adult. Admittedly the adult was very old and getting a bit feeble but it was a beginning, Karl thought. He had also begun to assert himself over his sister. One day she was standing on the carpet in the drawing room and he was in the music room. The two were divided by a brown velvet curtain, and a Persian rug lay halfway between each room. When he peeped through the curtain Karl saw her standing on the carpet and he pulled it and she fell down. She heard him laugh and rushed after him to box his ears, but Karl wasn't going to have his ears boxed any more. He squared up to her as Mr Charc had taught him and met her with a quick double blow, left, right, left. The poor girl had always dealt with Karl as if he were a soft jelly and made him squawk, then she had pinched him and that was that. But now the little monster was fighting back. He hit her again and again and she rushed off crying to her father, 'He has been beating me up and he even hit me on the breasts.' Karl did not see why he should not hit her anywhere he pleased and when he was told off he just replied, 'She's had it coming to her for many years.' To him it was the revolt of the oppressed against the cruel slavery of many years.

But now he had gut-ache, and he felt really ill. He told Grandfather Freudenberg that he was feeling unwell and he said, 'I'll call Dr Levi.'

'Let's see,' said Dr Levi when he came into the bedroom. He prodded Karl's stomach and it really was painful. 'It's appendicitis and you will have to be operated on. But your parents are in Switzerland and we can't reach them soon enough.'

Margot appeared from the background. 'That's quite all right, I'll assume responsibility, you go ahead and operate.' Karl thought to himself, this is her chance to get rid of me. He was desperately scared.

Although he had seen the hospital from the outside, he had never been inside. All he knew was what his mother had told him about her experiences in the war, and they seemed in the main to amount to operations and amputations. Dr Levi had once treated him with a red hot needle. Karl had stepped on a rusty nail in the builder's yard behind the garden and his foot was going red. His mother had said that they must go to Dr Levi because of the danger of blood poisoning. With good reason blood poisoning was dreaded and often Karl had read about the thin red line mysteriously moving up the limb and the patient struggling with fever, and then the cure, the miraculous cure. Dr Levi had heated a needle until it was red hot. 'Hold still,' he said gruffly.

'Hold on to me, darling, pinch me,' said Mutti. And then the needle went in and Karl gave a yell of pain and shifted his foot. Dr Levi was cross. 'Keep still, now you have moved and I have to do it again. Come on, let's see a bit of manliness.'

Karl was angry – as if it was his fault that he shifted his foot. He remembered the story of Mucius Scaevola who had put his hand into the red hot coals to show the Etruscans that he and all other Romans were not afraid. Anyhow, the needle went in a second time and there was a hiss, blue smoke and a smell of steak. It hurt so much that Karl could not even get a scream out and he just clutched his mother. As he did not get blood poisoning the family felt grateful to Dr Levi, and they always said to Karl, 'Without Dr Levi you would not be here any more.'

And now Dr Levi was sending him to hospital for an operation. Margot and Grandfather Freudenberg came into the room again. 'We have phoned your parents and told them they need not come, we will look after you.'

The ambulance came and Karl was carried out on a stretcher. He was gratified to notice that Ella was in tears and he braced himself to be 'good and brave'. In the hospital they put two leather straps over him and that frightened him more than anything; then came a gauze mask and someone said, 'You will be asleep soon,' and he struggled a bit, still saw the enormous lamp and then everything went out. He came round in a bedroom, puking into a kidney shaped bowl. He was sore but the next few days were good. There were visitors and everyone was nice to him. Cousin Joseph came: to Karl he seemed very grown-up indeed. He had black hair on his upper lip and he was working in the bank as an apprentice and he told Karl jokes.

It hurt Karl to laugh a lot but it was good to be the centre of interest. There was another man in the room who had had his leg amputated and he told Karl that though the foot had been taken off it was still hurting. He had been in the Great War and told Karl about it. He was not talking to a boy. He was a lonely man in pain who talked and talked about the trenches, how he had been muddy and lousy. 'Do you know,' he said, 'I used to sit there and squeeze the lice out of my shirt, one after the other; they came marching out towards me and it did not matter how many I killed, there were always more. They used to take us out of the front lines and take us to be cleaned up and all our clothes were baked in ovens to kill the lice.'

What hatred he had, seemed to be for the French, not the English soldiers. 'They had bully beef, that's why they won in the end. We went into their trenches and found tins of it, real meat, and they were giving us swedes and roasted acorns in our bread, and the coffee we had was made from roasted roots. They had white bread and, I tell you, they had thick red jam on their bread. They had everything and we were starving.' He groaned with pain and asked for his injection.

Karl was discharged after a few days and his sister fetched him home in a taxi. The hospital sister said 'You have got a smashing scar now, you were cut open by the best surgeon in Essen; come back in a fortnight to have the stitches taken out.'

Karl was helped to the taxi; he felt extraordinarily weak and cold. Inside the hospital all had been warm and cosy, now he was cold. He was put to bed in his own room. The bed felt huge and cold and he was afraid again. 'Don't think you will get anything special,' said his sister. 'You are better now and you must stop making a fuss.' Karl just wept in his huge bed and waited.

Mutti and Father came back from Switzerland at the end of the week and all was well again. His father brought him huge packets of stamps and his mother looked after him. 'You look pale and thin,' they said. Having for years teased him for being fat, all the family's energy now went on feeding him and getting him back to his old shape. At mid-morning Mutti brought him his second breakfast. The second breakfast had fortified his father and grandfather in their toil at the office. It was always something 'light', an omelette with herbs and a few delicate slices of white bread or possibly a slice or two of thin West-phalian ham, the speciality of the region. This was eaten with pumpernickel, very black, almost sweet rye bread, 'Do you know why they call it pumpernickel?' asked Grandfather Freuden-berg, 'it dates back to the time when the French invaded us in the wars with Napoleon. They said that that bread was 'bon pour un nickel' – only good for a rabbit. Well, we like it. My favourite way is to have a slice of white bread and a slice of pumpernickel, butter them both and put a slice of Westphalian ham in the middle and that's very good.'

For his convalescence Karl was made foamy, light omelettes and beef tea and he felt looked after and cherished. Since it was Ella in the kitchen now, Mutti dared to go in and she cooked more than she used to. Her friends thought this was taking the simple life a bit far. Every week she and two of her friends met for coffee and cakes. They had been schoolfriends, Martha and Margaret. Margaret had a long sharp nose, very thick, curly hair and a very sharp way of speaking. She had an unkind word for everyone, never missing a chance of saying something that made someone unhappy.

Mutti did not like either of them, and when the coffee party was over would regale the family with the awful things Margaret had said. When Karl was supposed to be out of earshot she also, once, said something about Margaret's husband 'having interests outside family life'. The tone of her voice implied something to do with sex. Mutti always censored anything to do with sex in front of Karl. It seemed to him that she talked more freely to Margot. Once there had been some talk about circumcision – 'not in front of the child' she begged. Karl thought this was a bit odd since he knew quite well that he had been circumcised. Grandfather Freudenberg had told him that 'the best circumciser in the whole district came over specially for you'. He knew it was something to do with religion and with his prick, which he looked at lovingly when he was alone. He had studied the pricks of men in the swimming baths and could see the difference, but what worried him most was that his was so small and that it had no hairs round it. The way the men were – that was the way to be, he could see that. He had planned to roll up a handkerchief and stick it into his bathing trunks in order to equal in status the real men in the baths.

Karl's mother had reddish auburn hair, and for a long time had worn it in a bun at the back of her head. Suddenly one day the bun was gone and her hair cropped. Karl hated the change, wept bitterly and was only consoled with a piece of green marzipan covered in chocolate. Afterwards, these sweets were known in the family as 'Garbo sweets' because the name of the hairdresser was Garbo.

The family had a lot of words just known to them, a secret code which confirmed their solidarity. There was also the family whistle. Mutti couldn't do it because she had never learned to whistle, but his father used it rather like a shepherd would. In a crowd the children knew where he was, or if they came out of a train the whistle would greet them before they could even see him; or Margot would whistle for Karl to hurry up when he was in the boys' changing room at Mr Charc's.

Mutti's hair was looked after by a hairdresser who came some mornings; this was in addition to the visits to Garbo. Karl knew when the hairdresser came because she heated her curling tongs over bars of solid methylated spirit tablets that burned with a quiet, blue flame, and she tested the right heat with strips of paper that curled but did not burn up. The smell of methylated spirit was nice, and he liked to go in and watch while there was women's business going on. He would sit very quietly and watch and listen, hoping to hear something interesting.

It was also worth while to be behind the velvet curtain in the other room when Mutti and her two friends were having their coffee. They took it in turns to entertain each other and there was obviously some competition, although there were also limits to what might be served as this was only coffee time. Mutti would prepare a many partitioned hors d'oeuvre dish and each glass partition had something different in it. There were shrimps, smoked salmon, Westphalian ham in thin slices, specially delicate ham made from loin of pork – this was oval and surrounded by a thin layer of fat – radishes, and salads of slices of ham, apple, celeriac and mayonnaise all mixed together.

Other visitors came in the evening. They were friends of both parents and on these occasions there would only be white wine, biscuits and fruit salad. Karl would be presented, bathed and in pyjamas, and would then go off to bed. Sometimes he would listen behind the door to hear what the grown-ups were talking about. It was often about the political situation, what one was to do and what others were up to. There was talk of emigration, where to go, if money could be taken and who might help. Some people had already emigrated for several reasons: the ones who were involved in some activity that the National Socialists disapproved of, like journalists and socialists, had got out straight away in 1933 when Hitler came to power. Now there was a growing trickle of those with money and foreign connections who decided to go. The Karpfs were a good example. Karl's father seemed to take the line, 'It's bad for us now but it may get better, we must change our ways and remain inconspicuous and the storm will pass. No one abroad will allow these maniacs to go too far.' When Father talked about 'changing our ways' he meant that Jews had not done enough manual work and had gone soft. They had deserted the values of their ancestors; but then he would also say, 'This is our country too. We have contributed and we helped to fight for it in the Great War. The Hartlands have done a lot for the town, look at the eye hospital.'

The eye hospital had been founded by a Hartland who had gone blind but felt a sense of gratitude to the medical profession. He was 'Secret Councillor Hartland'. When Karl asked what a secret councillor did his father said, 'Nothing. It is just a title they used to be able to buy from the Kaiser and it made them feel important.'

Titles were certainly in evidence; the other Hartlands, Lutz's parents, whom Karl visited, were doctors; not medicine Father explained, but Uncle Arnold had studied economics and now he was known as Herr Doktor Hartland and his wife was Frau Doktor Hartland.

Not long after the conversation about the eye hospital the plaque that commemorated the donation and mentioned the name Hartland was knocked off, instead of the inscription there remained a bare space and marks where the letters had been obliterated.

Karl had to play his part in changing the ways of the Jewish community by the style of his next holiday. He was sent to a holiday camp for Jewish children, like the one on Wyck but it seemed more stringent and demanding. Religion was much in evidence and Karl felt out of it because he did not know the rules of the orthodox religion. He was made to wear a little cap during meals. 'You are ignorant,' they said to him. 'Don't you know anything? You can't eat without a cap on.' Other transgressions followed; he asked for butter to put on bread that was to have sausage on it. 'Fool, you can't do that, where were you brought up.' There were prayers that he did not understand, and boys who did not like him because he seemed ignorant and spoiled. It was really a bit like school, only here Karl's crime seemed not being Jewish but not being Jewish enough. He frantically tried to get people to like him, but did not have much success. Someone made a joke just as Karl was drinking his vapid afternoon tea and he wanted to laugh uproariously to show that he appreciated a good joke, but the tea found its way up to the passage at the back of the nostrils and squirted out of his nose all over the wax cloth. 'You disgusting little pig, stand against the wall.' And he had to stand against the wall, an object of disgust. He was not allowed to go on eating his tea until the 'auntie' in charge said that he might do so.

The other disaster was Egon. Karl wanted to show that he was a man of the world and confided in him that he had seen his sister naked through the bathroom keyhole. Now he had never seen his sister naked, let alone through a keyhole, the geography of the bathroom made that impossible. Egon listened with interest. 'I think I ought to tell your parents about that,' he said. Karl was terrified, his power of reasoning left him completely. He should have worked out for himself that Egon did not know his parents' address and Karl certainly wouldn't have supplied it; or he might have worked out that Egon was just trying to make him feel bad. As Karl had made up the whole incident he felt guilty and just knew that he would do anything in the whole world to prevent Egon writing to his parents. 'Please don't write,' he begged, 'I'll give you some of my stamps. Egon graciously accepted the stamps but did not say whether he would write or not. Karl tried to avoid Egon but he would look for him and say, 'I'll tell them.' At the end of the week Egon suddenly left the home, without telling Karl and richer by several stamps and a good penknife.

The last week was enjoyable for Karl. He felt more accepted, had learnt the ways of the home and prayed with the best of them although he had no idea what he was actually saying. He could read Hebrew and though he had no understanding of the language at least he was able to hold the prayerbook the right way up. In his dormitory there were several boys more advanced in their sexual development than Karl and he envied them their splendid erections and their ability to hold a slipper on their erect penis and run the length of the room with it hanging from this peg. They told him that he would have one as long as that one day, but though he searched himself there was no sign of hair and he felt sadly deprived in the face of such splendid competition.

He came home feeling chastened and decided that he would reform himself and lead a good and religious life. He hummed the tunes of the Jewish songs he had sung and he made his own bed for several days. When his parents asked him if he had had a good time he said yes, and Mutti asked why he seemed a bit subdued. She bought him a new knife because he said he had lost his old knife, and he wondered if he would ever hear from Egon again. He carved several little boats out of the bark of huge fir trees and put them on his bedside table, where he had what he called his museum; several bits and pieces he had taken from downstairs, like a tiny cat family that sat round a silver table.

When Karl had visitors whom he wanted to impress he would take them to his museum and show his treasures. Everything in it he said was terribly valuable. The idea of having a museum came from his visits to the other Hartlands. The grey limousine still called occasionally and Karl was taken up there to play. When it had come to Karl's turn to invite Lutz he felt a sense of despair. 'This house is so small, I can't possibly invite him here,' he moaned to his father. 'You can always say the park opposite is part of the house,' said his father drily. In Lutz's house there were glass cupboards full of Egyptian fragments, stone statues and many paintings which Mutti said were extraordinarily valuable.

Mutti was not well. She had spots that turned into little blisters and then the blisters burst and left small areas of open raw flesh. She covered these with pieces of lint and bathed them with calamine lotion. There were also sore spots inside her mouth and she could not tolerate any food that had salt in it. It was miserable for her and the family who were not used to her being unwell. When Karl was alone with his sister he asked her what she thought of the illness. 'Of course it's serious, she is afraid she caught this illness off her own mother, and Father is doing all he can to convince her that it is a different thing; the trouble is that she knows enough about medicine not to believe everything she is told.'

With all the bits of bandage Mutti looked awful and was dispirited; about the only time she seemed cheerful was when Karl came to see her, and he told her stories about success at school which were completely untrue but it kept him talking and made him feel that he was doing something for her. He felt so useless. Margaret, the schoolfriend, visited, and when she left Mutti said, 'Well, she told me the dear lord doesn't let his trees grow into the sky!' She was furious with her friend and even Karl could see that Margaret was an utter cow. Obviously she had always been deeply jealous of the nice house and everything, and now was her moment of triumph. The gods had decided to punish the fortunate.

'Mutti is going into hospital for a little while,' said Father, 'they want to investigate what causes the infection and they may think of something to do.' And so she went into hospital.

Karl felt numb and just went to school, did what he was asked to there and took very little notice of what went on. He was not allowed into the great hall to hear Hitler's important broadcast, and with some of the other Jewish boys sat in the little prison. In the history lesson they were taught about the degradation of Germany in the Treaty of Versailles and how the time of revenge had come. The former bits of Germany that Hitler had reoccupied looked like a wolf with an open mouth on the map. 'We must shut the wolf's mouth, we must take a deep bite and take Czechoslovakia,' they shouted. Karl spoke. 'But what about the French treaty, won't this mean war and trouble for Germany?'

'Hark at Hartland,' said Brett, 'of course he would think only of abroad.'

The teacher was sarcastic; 'You seem to know a lot, you think you know better than the government. Would you like to be foreign minister?'

By that time Karl's face was a deep red and he neither could nor wanted to say any more. With his clenched fist he knocked underneath the desk three times and said the magic word and he did it down the stairs and all along the wall outside. They would see.

After school and his session with Mr Charc he went to see Mutti in hospital. She was with his father when he came in and he was sure she was getting better. She told him they were going to pull all her teeth out to get to the infection. It was said so lightly that Karl saw it as a minor step and they chatted about what sort of day he had had. He told her that he had been given a two in English. It wasn't true but it cheered her up. In fact the English lessons were not very good. A very small man, Mr Stoss, took them for English. He told them about England and made it sound as if the English talked with a mouth full of dumplings and all went to boarding schools and had a very splendid aristocracy. He said he wished Germany had their royal family back.

Father said to Karl, 'English is very important, you must learn as much English as you can. All the great businesses are there and it is a very fine country.' Karl accepted all that but what was difficult was to sit down and to learn words that meant very little to him. They were singing an English song – 'School is over, oh what fun, work is over and play's begun'. He sang it to his mother who looked delighted that her son had the voice of Caruso.

After they had taken all her teeth out they went on to another operation. 'It is internal,' said Father.

'It's the ovaries,' said Margot, 'they are taking them out because they can be the seat of infection.'

Mutti seemed much weaker after the second operation. After the teeth she had still made some jokes. 'Look at the splendid set of choppers they have made for me, aren't they beautiful? They are almost as good as Aunt Bertha's.' Aunt Bertha was the wife of Grandfather Freudenberg's brother. He, Father hinted, had married beneath himself. At any rate they once walked past some pretty miserable cottages on one of their Sunday walks and Father had said, 'That's were Aunt Bertha was born.' She was a formidable lady, corseted, with a small waist and she wore pince-nez glasses. Whether it was because of these glasses or her nature Karl did not know, but she seemed a pretty sour and bad-tempered lady. She was Grandfather Freudenberg's friend more than anyone else's and they kept each other company as both had lost their spouses. The thing about Bertha was that she was always on about her teeth and with less than even a sign of embarrassment she would take out her newly made false teeth and would show them around. Now in Essen, or at least in the Hartland social circle, talking about false teeth was about as good form as taking off one's rupture belt and handing it round. Everyone shook with horror and to Father it was just another proof that she was no lady.

After the second operation Mutti just lay there and did not seem to care about anything. Karl went away bewildered and just withdrew to his room, played with his museum pieces and fiddled with the wall at the point where he had poked at it so long that he had hollowed it out. The wallpaper had been torn off the mortar and the hole was big enough for about half his fist. It was underneath the bar on which the mattress lay and no one had noticed it. Karl had started making the hole after seeing a film about the Count of Monte Cristo, who had patiently dug himself out of his prison cell into that of a man with a huge beard who helped him to escape. If Karl went through his wall he would be in Ella's room.

Ella had been joined by another girl, Sophy. Sophy's brother had been in Karl's form at the Jewish elementary school. 'You remember my brother?' she said to him. Karl did. He had had red hair and his eyes were deep set into his face and were dark brown and seemed to flicker. When Mr Isaac had said 'Are there any poor boys in the class?' because there were some cabbages to give away, Sophy's brother's hand went up and Karl had felt embarrassed for him because he was poor, and for himself because he wasn't but he wanted a cabbage. He remembered his jacket. The sleeves seemed to be glued on. They were crumpled and there were ridge marks where the shoulder met the sleeve. 'You can always tell a good suit,' Grandfather Freudenberg had said, 'by the shoulders; the sleeve should fit there as if it had been poured on; and another thing, the buttons on the lapels should be real buttons with buttonholes.' So Karl never had much to do with Sophy's brother.

He got on well with Sophy, though; she was small and not much taller than he was and they used to scuffle together and wrestle. He was excited to find that he was much stronger than her and could throw her on the floor. Sophy squealed and laughed and Ella encouraged him. 'Go on rape her, she can do with it, she is asking for it, have a go.' Karl did not really know what she meant by raping, but he knew the phrase. It always came up in books about war. It was what French soldiers were said to have done to German womanhood, and he remembered a poster of a woman lying on the road with her legs in an absurd position and her skirt torn and it said underneath: 'French soldiers passed this way'.

Ella said, 'You will be a real menace when you grow up, we will all have to look out.' And Karl felt pleased at this. One morning he saw Sophy come out of the bathroom and she only had her knickers on. He was a bit surprised when she didn't want to wrestle with him, instead she shrieked and said, 'Go away or I'll tell your father.' She rushed into her room and turned her back towards him and pressed herself firmly into the corner. 'Get out,' she shrieked, 'I'll tell your father.' And she meant it. Karl retreated, a bit offended that she would not play with him.

It seemed to Karl that Mutti's illness went on and on. Why didn't she get better? He was angry with her for neglecting him and for having to make the trip to the hospital which he hated. He hated the smell and the room, and although the nurses were always nice to him he knew that they were really busy with other things. 'This is my boy, Karl,' Mutti would introduce him, and they would say they were pleased to meet him and what a big boy he was and then rush off.

Karl was taking more money from his father. He had progressed from the little money boxes in father's drawer to his back pocket. His father carried his paper money in a large wad in that pocket. When he called on him in the morning and he was already in the bathroom shaving, Karl would peel off a note from the wad, replacing the trousers carefully so that it looked as if they had not been disturbed. The snag was the button that was over the pocket. Some of his father's suits were harder to unbutton than others and sometimes his chewed fingertips were quite sore with the effort.

His father had stopped using cut-throat razors and now had 'safety razors' with blades. 'We will have to get one for you before long,' he said to Karl, 'and we will have to think about your barmitzvah.

It took a year to prepare a boy for the barmitzvah. The ceremony meant that as far as the Jewish community was concerned he was a man and could join the men's prayers, and it was reckoned that a child was no longer a child. Karl looked forward to it because he knew that everyone received grand presents and there was a great party. He went to the instructor at the synagogue and told him that it was time he was prepared for his barmitzvah. The teacher was also the 'cantor', the man who lead the singing. He was a gentle man with rimless glasses, slightly bald and worried looking. He was not a very good teacher, Karl thought, and he had rarely made the bible stories interesting or had inspired Karl with religious faith. He looked worried because he saw in Karl no great achiever of religious merit and his zeal had never impressed him. On the other hand Karl was a Hartland, and the Hartlands, particularly the other Hartlands, played a big part in the affairs of the Jewish community.

'Right, you must come into the class,' he said. 'First of all, when is your thirteenth birthday?' – it was still a long way away – 'and what tribe of Israel do you belong to?'

Karl had not got any idea what trible. 'Well, you can't be a Cohanime or your name would be Cohn or something like that.' Karl remembered the three men in the train who introduced each other. 'Kagan!' 'King!' 'Also Cohn!'

Many German Jews had changed their names in order to appear non-Jewish or to give their children a better chance in life. Often it did not work because they looked so un-German, and Jews claimed they could always spot another Jew. Perhaps they could, but as they never counted how many times they had been wrong there was little scientific validity to the belief. Certainly they would look at one another and think, 'Is he?' 'Surely with that nose he must be . . . ?' 'With a name like that, isn't he?' and in the same way they would list to each other the famous Jews. Or they would say of someone famous *'and* he is a Jew.'

Karl was not a Cohn. Was he a Levi? He could give no evidence that he came from the tribe of Levi. 'In that case you are of the tribe of Israel, the majority of people are of the tribe of Israel.' And so Karl became a member of the tribe of Israel. According to what tribe you were, the passage in the Torah was chosen. Reading from the sacred scrolls was a great honour, and the day of the barmitzvah was the boy's first reading. There could be no mistake, no stumbling or misreading. It all had to be word perfect or else the family would be in disgrace. Karl could not raise much enthusiasm for the classes; but he knew he had to learn to read a passage of Hebrew word perfect. The trouble was that in the proper Torah there would be no vowels under the Hebrew letters and without them reading would be much harder. So the boys had to learn their passage by heart, word perfect, and then read it, or rather pretend to read it when the great day came. Karl did not even know what the passage was about. He gathered it was from the book of Exodus but the cantor could hardly conceive that any boy of twelve could be as ignorant as Karl seemed to be, so he just set about his task by having him learn the passage for the great day.

Lutz joined the weekly class and the two would exchange glances and giggle until the cantor lost all patience and clipped

Karl over the head. Karl was outraged. A Hartland had been slapped by a minion! The cantor looked frightened. He had smacked a Hartland and without a doubt there would be trouble. However, it never occurred to Karl to report the matter. The disgraces at school and here were his problem and he did not expect support or understanding; he also realised that the cantor's exasperation was justified. But Lutz told.

'What happened at the synagogue?' his father asked.

'Nothing,' said Karl.

'Oh yes, something did. Look, you must behave in the classes. It is bad enough for the cantor having to take you lot without starting to muck about.'

Karl learnt the passage word perfect that evening and the rest of the year was spent repeating it and being let off after he had done it without a mistake.

Now that he had access to bigger sums of money Karl also became more ambitious in his spending. First there was the lending library. For the equivalent of a penny he could secretly borrow thrillers from a little lending library not far from the house. His father would not allow him to read trash.

'You must know the great literature of the world,' he would say. 'You should begin to read Shakespeare, he is even better in German than in English, they say. There were two great translators, Schlegel and Tieck, and you really should begin now. How about *Hamlet*?'

Karl cringed when he saw the text and was not helped when his father took to declaiming 'To be or not to be' in English. Learning the English verbs was bad enough.

When he found Karl with thrillers he was not pleased. 'Where did they come from? Why do you want to read rubbish like that? Watch out. *Facile est descendere in Averno.*'

To Karl the thrillers did not seem like rubbish. He read them at feverish speed and changed one or two each day. He put the books down on the steps by the cellar door at the side of the house, went to the front door empty-handed and innocent, and then fetched the books up to his room. They were covered with special paper. It was called parchment and one could see the title through it. The books were rather dirty and yellow.

'Why bother with those filthy things,' Father had said. 'Look, we have two huge cases full of books in the drawing room, you can read those if you want to.'

But those weren't about the war and prisoner-of-war camps in France, where all the prisoners were lusting after the commandant's wife. They weren't gangster stories where the murderer committed his crime by attaching himself to a helium balloon and shooting through the fourth floor window or got rid of his opponents' leader, impregnable in a penthouse flat, by feeding poison into the water supply. There were stories translated from the English, and Karl was greatly puzzled by the heroine who held on to the hero's unmentionables; what was unmentionable? If it was his prick could she have held on to it. Margot settled the problem by saying it was probably the man's underpants because the English were funny that way. They would not even mention the word underpants. She had been told that they put knitted covers over piano legs.

Chapter 6

Karl came home from school in his usual slow way: first the sweets, then the column with the murder posters and advertisements on it, and then he changed his route and went along the main road where the shops were. He looked into the window of Koenig's, the caterers. They had held a competition in praise of their coffee; the prize was an ocean cruise and Karl wanted to enter because he liked the idea of a cruise; he had read about Colonel Fawcett's mysterious expedition up the Amazon so he asked his father to help him with the couplet and he came out with

> *Always give Koenig's coffee a miss*
> *Because it tastes like warmed up piss*

so the competition never came to anything.

The air gun shop was another good place to stop for a look, then there was a pet shop and then a cake shop. It was a slow walk and he only got a move on when he realised that he might miss lunch.

Ella opened the door. Her eyes were red and she said, 'Go upstairs and see your father.' What have I done wrong now? thought Karl as he rushed up the stairs and then he realised that it had to be something to do with his mother. His father was standing with his back to him in the upstairs living room.

'I am afraid your mother died this morning. She was very ill and suffered a great deal and it was the best thing for her.' He just about said it all and at the end his voice gave a little squeak and he stood very still facing the window again. Karl went to another window. He did not know what to say. He wanted to rush up to his father and clutch him but he couldn't, so he said 'Can I see her?' and his father said 'No. The funeral will be on Wednesday.' 'Can I come?' 'Yes.' Karl cried for a bit but it wouldn't come out; he wiped his nose on the net curtain and for at least a year the dried out bit of snot remained on the curtain and reminded him of her death.

'I told Ella to serve lunch downstairs,' said Father, 'so that we can be with Grandfather Freudenberg.' And so they went down. When Grandfather saw Karl and his father he gave a howl of anguish, a desperate cry, and then he sobbed and sobbed. Karl had never seen an adult cry before and it frightened him. It was also the first time that he realised other people loved his mother. Once she had been his entirely and then she had become more remote in her illness and he had made himself forget that she wasn't there and that he missed her. Karl had to rush out of the room and he went to his bedroom and threw himself on his bed and he cried; and then he got out one of his 'bad' books and read it intensively and felt guilty at the same time that he was doing anything else but grieving. There was a knock on the door and his sister came in. 'Come on downstairs, you must be hungry.' She was nice to Karl and he knew she was as miserable as he was. The girls in the kitchen were crying. 'She was a good woman,' said Ella. There was a rush of activity. The doorbell rang, telegrams came and everyone seemed busy. Relatives were asked to come to the funeral and many things had to be arranged. Notices were inserted in the daily paper and Karl was told that he need not go to school.

He retreated to his room, reading his books. He got through two in the afternoon and he went through his box of secret treasures. He had bought another gun for himself. It was a reproduction of a colt revolver and it was heavy and looked like a real gun. It fired brass caps and there were special caps with tear gas in them. It said on the box that these could be used against burglars and for self-protection. Karl had tried out the gun with Lutz when he went to his home for one of his visits. They had fired it so close to their ears that when they sat down to tea they were half-deaf and their ears were singing. Karl could not play with this new gun at home because someone might have asked him how he got the money for it and it had cost the sort of money that wasn't just found lying on the pavement. Karl had made up his mind that if anyone asked him about the gun he would say that he had borrowed it from a schoolfriend.

When he came down for supper everything was a bit calmer. The grown-ups had controlled their grief and were now occupied with practicalities. Margot was going to organise the food after the funeral and they worked out who would come, and who would come for the food but not the funeral. Margot was to stay at home and wait for the men when they came back and a taxi had been ordered specially for the family. Dr Weil was going to take the service. Dr Weil was the rabbi for the Jewish community. Mutti had said of him that he was known as the other Hartlands' private chaplain. Certainly as Uncle Arnold was the head of the community the appointment of the rabbi would have very largely depended on his vote. Also Dr Weil and his family were frequent guests at the home of the other Hartlands. Karl knew one of his daughters because he had lifted up her skirt in the playground and been told off for it when he was in the elementary school. Dr Weil had very big heavy cheeks that seemed to hang down at the sides. He wore thick, very thick spectacles, and Karl remembered him mostly with a black, high, square rabbi's hat on. He preached every Saturday and his voice rose to dramatic heights but Karl did not understand a word he said, and just watched his arms waving about. When Dr Weil finished preaching, the organ would start up magnificently and he got off his preaching perch amidst magnificent sounds.

The next morning the notification of the death appeared in the papers. It was a large notice but not as big as some people had. Some people had a whole page. With Mutti, it was a quarter of a page. It said that Gertrude Elisabeth Hartland had departed from this life and that her death was mourned by her close family; then it gave Father's, Grandfather's and the children's names. It was a simple notice, not showy like some of the others which had palm leaves across them or broken-off columns. 'Jewish people don't go in for that sort of showiness,' said Father. 'Jewish funerals are very simple.'

Karl was told to buy himself a piece of black crêpe as an armband. Some people sewed black triangles on their arm but his was going to be an armband.

First there was a service in the synagogue. Dr Weil mounted his high platform and gave a funeral oration. Mutti did not sound like a real person any more but an angel who had been a good daughter, a nurse in times of war, a mother to her children and a good wife to her husband. There were prayers and then Karl, his father and others left for the graveyard. They went there in cars and they got out by the great gas-holder and walked towards the black cast iron gate of the cemetery. It was a bitterly cold day and everything seemed grey and bleak. 'Now we have to be very brave,' said Father as they trudged to the chapel. Grandfather Freudenberg just stared ahead and said nothing, and Karl could not bear to look at his father. Inside the chapel he saw his mother in a small pine box. He could see it was pine because the end was left uncovered and over the rest there was a white sheet. Now there were no pompous orations, just the prayer for the dead and then the coffin was picked up and carried towards the grave. Karl looked down into the grave and there was the box, right at the bottom. His father was given a little shovel and put three shovelfuls of earth on to the coffin. Then it was Grandfather's turn and then Karl's. The earth made a loud plopping noise as it fell on the coffin lid. A bit of the lid was already covered by the time the man after Karl had put his lot on. After that all the mourners filed past the coffin, put some earth in and then shook Father's, Grandfather's and Karl's hand. The worst thing for Karl was seeing the pine box when he first came into the chapel. She is in there, he said to himself, and she will never get out again.

At home Margot had organised the coffee and the cake and the various salads. Bertha was there and so were Martha and Margaret. They were all talking in an animated way and suddenly Bertha reached into her mouth and took her dentures out.

97

Martha disappeared from the room and so did Margot. Karl heard giggles outside and went to look. They were both helpless with laughter, tears were streaming down their faces they were laughing so much. At first Karl felt guilty because he knew that this was a sad occasion and that he was supposed to be serious, but this was too much. 'I knew she would do it,' said Martha, 'I knew it. I should have made a bet with you and I would have won it,' she gasped.

The next day Karl went back to school, the black crêpe band draped round his arm. The music teacher rushed up to him. 'Who has died, my boy?' 'My mother,' Karl said, and he replied, 'Oh, it is dreadful, losing your mother when you are so young,' and Karl felt mellow and slightly important. Everyone left him alone and nothing else was said.

Karl sat quietly in his corner hoping that someone would take notice of him. When he had come back from his appendicitis operation he had for a time attracted some attention because he was able to show his scar. He was excused PT because of the operation and he sat in the back of the gym and said how sad he was to miss the exercises. Once the stitches had been taken out there wasn't much left to boast about and he had been able to demonstrate his utter incompetence at jumping over the horse again.

But the lessons with Mr Charc still went on. 'I'll make a champion out of you,' said Mr Charc. 'I'll develop your muscles and we'll put you in for weight-lifting competitions.' Every week another black disc was added to the steel bar and Karl pushed it up with much grunting, pulling and heaving. There were three ways of lifting weights up: first by pushing, when the arms were straight; then secondly the weights could be 'torn' up from the ground in one mighty pull, at the same time planting the feet apart; and thirdly the weights were pushed up, but at the same time the legs helped by giving an additional push. 'Legs apart and push,' Mr Charc would shout and Karl pushed. He was shown to other students as the star, the boy who lifted more weight than anyone else. The other students included grown-ups, mostly rather stout ladies; but there was one Karl thought was very beautiful. 'She is a barmaid,' Margot whispered to Karl. Obviously, that was an evil thing to be. She added, 'I don't think she pays her fees, Mr Charc makes her pay in other ways!' Most of the time Karl had lessons by himself, but he was in a group for boxing and they all belted into one another and it did not hurt too much because the gloves were huge. Mr Charc's knuckles were covered in thick hard skin. 'That comes from working on the sand bag.' He would throw Karl the thin gloves and send him over to hit a kitbag full of sand hanging from the ceiling.

Mr Charc never handed anything over slowly, everything was thrown. He was always in motion, weaving pushing and punching his imaginary opponent. 'One-one-two,' he would gasp. 'Come on, you are Schmelling and I am Louis,' and they would batter away at one another very happily until the sweat was running off both of them. Schmelling was the German boxing hero who had defeated the brown bomber, Joe Louis, in their first match but the second time round Joe Louis had knocked him out within seconds. When the news reached school everyone was furious. 'It was a foul,' they shouted, 'he hit him in the kidneys and that's definitely a foul.' It was as bad as when Jesse Owens, also a negro, had won the hundred metres race in the Olympics. The boys were taught that negroes were an inferior race. Karl knew what it must be like to be a negro because he was thought of in the same way. The logic seemed to be: 'You are useless at PT, therefore all Jews are useless at physical exercise.' So he had some sympathy for Owens and Louis. He had never seen a negro. Mutti had told him that when Margot was four they had taken her to a show at the exhibition hall opposite the house and in a war dance a huge negro had waved his spear at her, laughing, and shouting 'Tegelac tegelac,' and Margot was led out screaming her head off. There was a story he had heard: a negro sits in a café in the middle of the town and man comes up to him, bends over him and asks in a confidential voice, 'Are you from Essen?' The negro says, 'No,' and the man walks away saying, 'Ah that's why.' Karl also wondered if we, the Jews, are thought to be so inferior why do they bother to warn everybody about us, talking about the menace of impure blood and the defilement of German womanhood?

After Mutti's funeral, when the letters of condolence had been answered, life settled down to a kind of routine. Grandfather Freudenberg was in charge of running the house and Father went back to the bank, and as far as they could they went on as before.

'Will you fetch Mutti's suitcase from hospital?' Father said a few days after the funeral. 'They have phoned up and it is ready for collection.'

In the afternoon Karl went to the ward his mother had been in and asked if he could have the suitcase, please. The sister wore a blue dress and her cap was starched and rose behind her head like a pigeon's tail. She took Karl to a store room. 'Isn't it too heavy for you?' she asked, but Karl said, 'No it's quite easy,' and he managed to lift it. 'Well, off you go then, goodbye.' He trundled the case down the steps.

The smell of disinfectant brought Mutti back. He remembered his visits to the hospital, the little lint squares, and he remembered that Father had given Mutti a handful of fifty pfennig pieces and she had put them into a purse: 'Just in case you need some small change.' And Karl made up his mind to look for the money when he got home.

The trip home was a nightmare. The case was large, made of thick brown pigskin, and it seemed to be packed full with clothes. Karl pulled it behind him, he changed hands more and more often and he was sweating. He had to walk because the tram line did not go directly back to his home, and it did not occur to him to take a tram into the centre and then another out to his house.

He got home with his hands sore and blistered and angry with his father for making him carry the case. He took it into the dressing room, a sort of ante-chamber to his parents' bedroom. The wardrobes were built in and inside the doors were huge mirrors. There were drawers upon drawers, one for collars, one for underwear, one for scarves, and each drawer had a label on it to tell what was supposed to be in it. His father's wardrobe had his suits in it. On the first hanger was his velvet smoking jacket. He always put it on when he came home in the evening. It was black velvet and very old and comfortable. He lost his look of stiffness when he put it on. All the things the children might need were in his pockets: a huge rubber which had been in there for a long time, it was shiny and black; a penknife, a round pencil sharpener and often steel clips and rubber bands. Karl would go to the wardrobe to borrow whatever he needed, even when his father was not wearing the jacket. There was also a dressing table. This was where Mutti used to sit when the hairdresser curled her hair, and there was a couch for afternoon naps. Karl put the case on the couch and opened it. The purse was in the pocket inside the back of the case. It was a black purse and it was full of money so he took the lot. He shut the case again and left it.

'I see you brought the case back,' said his father in the evening. 'Was it very heavy?' Karl said it had been heavy but that he had managed and his father said, 'I thought you would.'

Every morning Grandfather went out to do the shopping. He carried the vegetables in a net and they would all hang out and look untidy. The greengrocer's was not far away and he would shop for bargains. Karl hated to go shopping with him because he felt embarrassed when Grandfather *would* ask what was cheap that day. Here we live in that big house with trees round it and the old fool asks what is cheap; he is as bad as Aunt Julia. Aunt Julia was Joseph's grandmother. Her white hair stuck out in all directions as she dragged a huge net of vegetables and groceries from the central market back home. She talked very quickly and giggled between words. She called Karl 'my little boy' which he didn't like, and what was worse she made him kiss her stubbly chin and she gave him biscuits that smelt funny. Margot thought that she stored the biscuits under her dirty underwear and that was why they were not a bit like the biscuits at home. It was also possible that she had bought remainders at the market and over the weeks they had lost their crispness. Her daughter, Cecilia, was also a bit eccentric. 'It's because of the war,' Mutti had said of her. 'She is so scared of being short of food that she can't bear to throw any of it away.' It was true. In her kitchen there were innumerable pots with food in them, they stood everywhere and Karl did not like eating there. They had to at times, and he and his father went there full of foreboding. 'When you were little,' his father told him, 'one day after supper you climbed under the table and you said you would rather sit there than eat any of that cake, and we could not really tell you off because we knew exactly what you meant; but still they are family and she is doing her best.' They went to eat more frequently at Cecilia's after Mutti's death. She felt that the family needed proper nourishment and support. She was nice to Karl and she would open her boy's toy cupboard and he was allowed to play with his meccano set.

Suddenly Father asked Karl if he wanted an air gun. Karl had wanted an air gun as long as he could remember. He knew them all. The beautiful rifles with polished stocks and dull gun metal barrels. 'You will have to be careful with it, air guns can be dangerous.' Karl hotly promised that he would be careful and that he would look after the gun. 'You must never point it at anyone and when you walk with it it must be broken open so that it can't be fired by mistake.'

The air gun came and Karl loved it. It fired little bolts with feathers at the end and when it had been fired there was a smell of dry dust. And it fired lead pellets. Karl fixed a paper target on a board and all the family took turns to fire at the paper target. When he was alone he grew more ambitious, he opened the window, stood a toy soldier on the wooden ledge and soon he had shot his damaged and spare soldiers to pieces. The window ledge was pitted with little black holes and the wood was beginning to splinter. All the damage was covered up when the window was closed. He fixed targets to the wall in his room and then peppered them with pellets. In the garden he lay behind bushes and shot at imaginary enemy soldiers who were crawling towards him. He fired from the hip, he fired from the shoulder and right at the back of the garden he dug himself a trench. There had been a flower garden but the flowers had not come to much.

Most of the gardener's time just went on the lawn, the rose beds and the front of the house. In all this neglected space Karl had his secret places. He dug as deep as he could and soon reached stone and rubble. He covered a corner with boards and made a hut of sorts. From the back garden he could climb into the builder's yard and there he found a good supply of materials. Except for his appendix Karl had got all his scars in the builder's yard. No one ever saw him there and he did his damage quietly but persistently. Old window frames had their panes broken; inside huts he turned bags of cement over and he trampled on the sand pits. He looked at the lime pits with terror and respect. He had been told that anyone who fell in would be gone for ever, boiled up by the acid.

In the annexe to the yard lived old Fritz and sometimes Karl visited him. He was a very old man, so old that his face was all wrinkles. He smoked herbal tobacco and in his tiny room there was very little furniture, just an iron bed, a table and a little washstand. He said that he had been in the battle of Sedan and Karl desperately wanted to know what it had been like. 'We had very hard black bread,' he said, 'nowadays I could not chew it, like little hard bricks, and they gave us little pieces of fat bacon to go with it, and if we were quartered anywhere we had bean soup or lentil soup. If you had been marching a long time and you got sore between the legs then you would take a bit of bacon fat and rub it in your crotch. One dirty sod gave a piece to his mates to eat after he had used it; when they had eaten it he said, "Yes, it is good. I have been rubbing it in my crotch for days." The French, they were rich; white bread, wine everywhere; as we used to say "They live like gods in France." I was with the horses, used to pull carts. I did not hate the French; they are just like us, poor sods. But we won the war and now they want their revenge.'

He showed Karl his belt. The buckle had the imperial German crest on it, and he also had his old bayonet which he brought out like a treasure. 'Did you ever use it?' Karl asked. 'No I just used it for roasting potatoes,' Fritz said.

If things got worse in the house after Mutti's death, it was a gradual business. Little things that went wrong were not put right. Grandfather would tell the 'ladies' as he called them, and they would laugh. 'Stupid old fart' Ella would say, and Karl thought that was very funny. He told Ella about the little cloth and she would say poor old shit, he is past it. There were quite a few people the girls felt contempt for and whose lives they must have made miserable. One was old Cohn who came with the bread. Once a week he would call with a huge suitcase full of bread and they would buy a couple of loaves whether they needed them or not. Cohn had been in the artillery in the Great War and he had lost his hearing. 'The chairisch [deaf] old idiot is here,' Karl would announce, and one of the girls would rush out, get the money from Grandfather and then call out, 'How is it then, Mr Cohn, getting it regularly are you? Still at it, old shithead?' and they would roar with laughter and he would nod and laugh and the more outrageous the question he said yes to, the more they would laugh. 'I don't know,' said Ella, 'if I was in that position I would put a bullet through my head. Fancy lugging a case full of bread around, for God's sake. I ask you, what can you make on a few loaves of bread.'

Another regular caller was little Miss Schmidt, who had some connection with the family. She had been housekeeper of one of Father's cousins and Karl gathered that possibly it had been a somewhat closer relationship. She had been left a pension which she drew from Karl's father through the bank, and she brought ground coffee. She carried a suitcase and when she opened it there was a marvellous smell of coffee. On special occasions she brought cheese-cake and it was the best cheese-cake there has ever been. It was neither too sweet nor too sour, not sticky and not sickly. No one minded that her squat fingernails were deep black and her hands grey rather than pink. Her cheese-cake was very special.

Still another caller was the egg man who aroused no comment from anyone. He came all the way from Holland with his eggs. He had started to come over the frontier after the war when food had been really short, and he carried his eggs in a high wicker basket that went up right above his head. The eggs lay between layers of hay and when he sold them they were put into wooden trays with holes in them. The eggs then went into the larder which Ella kept locked.

The main reason she locked it was to keep Karl out. He went for everything edible and she said, 'How can I plan ahead with you eating everything?' Sometimes Karl found the keys in her apron pocket, and he became very skilled at taking food so that no one would notice he had done it. He would just cut a few slices off the salami, spoon off the top of the herring salad and then replace the decorations, or he would just munch up dry pieces of 'pea sausage'. This was dehydrated pea soup packed like a sausage. When mixed with water again it would make pea soup. 'When the war broke out,' his Grandmother Hartland had told him, 'there were two things you had to do: collect together gold coins and pea soup sausages.'

Quite often beggars came to the door. They were given thick slices of bread with margarine in between. 'Not butter,' Ella said with authority. They were never given money. 'If you give them money they keep on coming back; give them something to eat and then they won't feel they have been refused.' At one time coupons were kept and given to the beggars and each coupon entitled the caller to a meal in the centre of town. When coke was delivered in the front of the house there would be one or two men who came very timidly to ask if any help was wanted with shifting the coke into the cellar. This work was the prerogative of the Rademacher family, and when the coke had come it was Karl's job to go to the house and tell them that the coke had to be shifted, Mr Rademacher still called every morning and did the boiler and then went on to his next job. He was bald and very thin, everything in his face was stretched downwards and he had huge strong hands. Karl liked to watch him fill the boiler with coke. He was marvellously skilful and not one piece of coke went astray. It all shot straight into the red inferno, exactly where he wanted it. Now that he was stronger and bigger Karl tried his hand at getting the coke into the boiler and he became good at it. He loved the cellar where the boilers were. There were two huge ones for the winter and a smaller one for the summer. When the coke was shovelled into the store he would help, either filling the barrows or standing by the chute watching the coke go down, and he would slide down the chute himself, enviously watched by Mr Rademacher's son, Heini, who was not allowed to get his clothes dirty.

Karl slowly learned what it meant not to have money. It meant you could not do what you wanted on the spur of the moment but you had to think ahead. Father was pleased that Karl helped with the coal. 'He must learn to put his hand to anything,' he would say to Grandfather Freudenberg. Karl preened himself. Not only was he doing something useful, he was growing up. His voice varied its pitch and sometimes it came out quite deep and sometimes he squeaked. 'Like a young bull,' said Grandfather Freudenberg, 'he roars like a young bull.' Karl had also noticed some curly hair round his prick which now seemed a better size. 'I will be able to take part in the slipper race next year,' he said to himself.

Plans for the barmitzvah were made. 'It won't be right without your mother,' said Father, 'but we must go on.' By now Karl knew his passage word perfect and the cantor told him all would go very well indeed and he would be a credit to his family. 'What is more you will be able to say the prayer for the dead for your poor mother,' he added. All of the close family were invited and it meant a great long table full of guests. Flora and Julius from Aix-la-Chapelle had to be put up for the night, and there were the guests from Berlin. Margot was no longer at home. She had begun a course in fashion design in Berlin and seemed to Karl more and more sophisticated every time she came back. She even wore make-up and she was so grown up she did not hit him any more. Occasionally she tried to be in charge and would complain about Karl's uncouth feeding habits and his filthy underwear, but did not go on quite so persistently any more. Perhaps she realised it was hopeless.

After the ceremony there was going to be a big luncheon at the Hartland house. A special cook was engaged and prepared dishes were sent up from the caterers. First there was to be clear soup with little egg dumplings; then various salads, and after that venison in a thick burgundy sauce, followed by a bombe of ice cream. Before Karl went to the synagogue with his father he looked into the dining room and he knew it was going to be magnificent. More tables had been brought in and all the extra leaves had been put into the ordinary table. There were piles of table linen and napkins. The silver had been polished the day before. Silver polishing was done every fortnight, and the maids and the extra helper would sit by a table and each piece would be covered with a pink cream. This was rubbed off and then the piece was polished with a soft cloth. It always seemed a jolly occasion, and when they had finished, the various silver pieces looked shiny and magnificent. There was the tea set that stood on the dining room sideboard, dishes, knives, forks and spoons. Each had a baroque design and seemed rather heavy and ponderous.

When the right moment came in the synagogue, Karl was called forward. The holy scriptures had been brought out of their cupboard and had been held high and their various vestments had been taken off. Karl sat on a little bench and piece after piece was read out and then came his turn. He was wearing his prayer shawl for the first time. It had long threads at each corner, it was made of wool and had an off-white colour. First he had to take a corner of his shawl, touch the scriptures with it and put it to his mouth. Then he read, and his reading was guided by a marker which was shaped like a pointing finger. Karl made no mistakes and the honour of the family had been preserved. He was then stood in front of Rabbi Weil who hovered over him with his huge gown made of black stuff and his square black hat. He rejoiced in admitting Karl into the community as a man, gave an account of the family history, and dwelt at length on the recent and tragic death of his mother. He spoke of the good work his father was doing and the distinguished past of his grandparents and the contributions all the Hartlands had made, and said finally that they were all about to enter into difficult and testing times. He blessed Karl by stretching his rather podgy hands over him and opening them so that he made a V sign with two fingers on each side. The ceremony seemed to be over and they all went out. Many shook Karl by the hand congratulating him on his splendid and manly performance. He went home on the tram with Aunt Flora, who had come to the service without her husband who probably kept to his principles and refused to go near a synagogue. They talked about Mutti; Flora said that she had been a happy and humorous little girl and that once she stuck both her knees into her nightgown and said, 'Now I have got big breasts like you.' She asked Karl how things were and what he was doing. Again Karl felt that here he was talking to an adult who understood him and he felt happy. At home a pile of presents was waiting for him. The other Hartlands had sent him a stopwatch. He did not know what to do with it. Several times he held his breath to test how long he could.

The presents were not really meant to give pleasure; they were the equipment of a cultured young man about to embark on adult life. There were volumes of Goethe, Schiller and other 'good' writers. Karl never opened them but they looked impressive on his bookshelf. There was a big leather attaché case, a leather writing table set, together with an ebony letter opener. A watch, several pens and a small, very fine leather suitcase. The only present he really liked was a camera and his father gave him that. Everyone looked at the presents and said what a lucky chap he was and how well he had read his piece. Then lunch. The table looked magnificent: the crystal glass had been brought out, all the silver dispayed and for each place setting there were as many silver knives, forks and spoons as courses. The knives rested on silver knife rests and there were flowers on the table. 'Only one glass of each wine,' said his father to Karl, and that was all he had; in fact at the end of the meal he felt that he had not done as well as when he went foraging in the kitchen on his own. Then he stood wearing his deep blue serge suit with, for the first time, long trousers, black shiny shoes and a tie. His father had lent him one of his many silk ties. Speeches were made and everyone drank a toast to Karl who had nothing left in his glass. He heard his Aunt Cecilia say to her neighbour 'I got rid of the maid when Joseph had his barmitzvah; after that it wasn't safe any more to have her in the house.' Karl pricked his ears up and wondered what he was missing and would the maids in his house go because of him. Ella had said he was going to be a menace soon; how exactly could he be a menace, he wondered. He had to stand up, and say that he was grateful for all his presents and that it was the best day in his life, that he wanted to say thank you to all, and that was all he had to say. There was much laughter and applause and they said if only poor Gertrude could have heard him, it would have been the happiest day of her life.

After coffee and cake they left. Everyone had turned gloomy. 'This is the last time the whole family will be together like that,' said Flora prophetically. 'It's all coming to an end; those scoundrels are out to spoil everything.' There had been much talk about the possibility of emigration; where one could go and what one could do. Countries that Karl knew only from stamps were mentioned – Uruguay was good for visas; had they heard that in Argentina you could settle if you had enough dollars. They told the story of Bella. Everyone agreed that she was the real beauty of the family. She had lived in Berlin and had dressed really well. She had married but was divorced. She discovered that she had a right to US citizenship because somehow or other she had been born on an American ship. She claimed her citizenship and waited and waited, and then she gave up and took an overdose of veronal and the next day the visa came! The family took leave of one another and Karl was left with his magnificent presents, a prayer shawl, and the thought that he now could say the prayer for the dead for his mother.

A few days after the barmitzvah his father said to him, 'How about a dog? Shall we buy a dog?' Karl was so pleased he was almost beside himself. To own a dog, a dog of his own. He went quite red and asked his father if he really meant it. Sometimes his father had teased him in the past and it had hurt. The first time was when Karl was alone in the living room and the phone rang. Karl loathed the telephone. He was physically afraid of it and would sweat profusely when he had to talk on an outside line. There was a phone in the drawing room, one in the living room, one in the passage outside the kitchen and another one in his parents' bedroom. By pressing a button on top and turning a handle on the side it was possible to phone from one room to another. For outside calls there was a dial. When the phone rang Karl thought it was an outside line and he picked up the receiver nervously. 'This is President Hindenburg,' a deep voice said, 'I want to come and have dinner with you and your family. I want broad beans and bacon for my lunch. Would you please tell your parents?' Karl said, 'Yes, Mr President, I will tell my parents,' and trembling with excitement he rushed into his parents. 'It was Hindenburg and he wants to have lunch with us and he wants broad beans with bacon!' Broad beans with bacon was the one food Karl hated. His parents looked at him and then they burst out laughing and Karl knew he had been caught out and he was furious. As a revenge he put a whoopee cushion under his father's cushion on the chair he sat on for lunch. When there was a loud farting noise as he sat down Karl was a bit surprised that his father and mother were cross and that he was sent out of the room.

So he had to make absolutely sure about the dog; this was too serious a matter for foolery. They looked in the paper for advertisements for dogs, and went to a number of houses to look at the dogs advertised. First they saw a terrier. 'It must be a small dog,' said Father, 'and it must not leave hair everywhere.' The terrier did not appeal, and eventually they saw an advertisement for an Alsatian. 'Let's just have a look,' said Karl. They found the salesman and his kennel in the deepest slums of the town. The dog was kept in a hutch at the back of a high tenement where the plaster was peeling off and there was a smell of piss. The man who sold the dog was a cringing and excessively respectful man. 'Wounded in the war, sir, fought at Verdun all the way through, please remember I fought at the front.' The dog was beautiful, an Alsatian with a black back and sand coloured paws and big ears. 'You can tell he is pure, sir, look at his tail, look at his ears.' Pure Alsatians had ears that stood up like starched triangles of fur and their tails curved down and up in a gentle sweep. 'Could we see the pedigree?' asked Father.

'Sorry, it's not available at the moment, but we will post it on; he certainly has a good pedigree. I am only asking forty marks for him.'

'Twenty,' said Father.

Karl felt embarrassed at his father risking the chance of buying such a beautiful animal for a mere twenty marks, but the man said twenty-five; they shook hands and a long-haired Alsatian was theirs. He had a rope round his neck and the first thing they did was to buy a collar, a lead and a special bowl for his food. The dog hadn't been trained at all and pulled whoever was holding the lead all over the place.

Ella looked suspicious when they came home. 'I don't like dogs and if he craps anywhere who will clean it up?'

'I will,' Karl promised, and at that moment he meant it.

The first thing the dog did was to pee on the carpet. 'We must get him into the garden quickly.' And Karl not only had to mop up the mess, but Ella told him to sprinkle coffee on the stain to stop the smell.

Karl had two names for the dog. The official one was Hasso, but he also called him 'Pisser'. He loved the dog and everyone else hated him. Margot was disgusted when she came from Berlin for a weekend. 'How could you?' she said to Father. 'He will mess the place up and Karl will never look after him. There are already hairs everywhere; at least he should be kept off the good chairs.'

The dog slithered over the lino and made worse scratches on it than Karl; every rug seemed to give way under him and he crashed against the walls. But he barked, no doubt about that; he barked every time the bell rang and any time a car or anything else passed on the road outside. It was so chaotic that Father had him sent to a training school and he came back a week or two later a relatively reformed character. He would sit when told to, would walk on a lead and not pull on it and he would not jump on anybody. Nevertheless there were lapses. Ella opened the door when Karl came home from school. 'Look what your friend has left for you,' and she led Karl to a vast pile on the stair carpet. He was lucky she didn't rub his nose in it. He cleared it away, though, and he fed the dog. Every day he consumed a wash bowl of rice and dog meat and if anyone came near him while he was eating he would growl dangerously.

Karl felt wonderful; this was his dog, everyone else was afraid of him, but he loved him. He would sit for ages cuddling and stroking him, inventing new names and singing to him, 'My friend animoso, good beastie, my doggie faced pissy dog,' and the beast just looked contented. They went for walks and people would step off the pavement to avoid brushing past the dog – and Karl liked that. The only snag was that when Karl was in school the dog was locked on the balcony outside the bathroom and he howled and barked. One day the phone rang. 'Would you shut the damned Jew dog up, it's making too much noise.' Boys on the other side of the wall in the parking lot would call for Karl. There had always been trouble about that. 'I don't want you to play with gutterboys,' his father said to him. Once they had called over, 'Give us some fruit, chum,' and Karl had handed over a huge pear which the family had been watching grow. Lately the boys had been less friendly. 'Jew boy come on over,' they called and sometimes a stone came over. Karl got very excited when they shouted to him because he was so lonely and he would have loved to have someone to play with. But an old lady called one day and told Ella, 'The boys are planning to take your boy and tie him to a tree and whip him. I thought I should tell. I don't think it is right.' Karl was firmly told to stay indoors, and that evening hordes of boys on bicycles roared round the car park. Sometimes they called, 'Come on out, come and play,' or 'Why aren't you coming to play? You promised.' Some of the boys had torches and Karl was so scared he lay on the floor of his room and didn't dare to move.

One morning Father said, 'The other Hartlands have gone! They went without telling anyone and without saying goodbye and left everything behind; and then Rabbi Weil and his family left just as suddenly. Father was obviously depressed about these departures, which left the Jewish community leaderless, until two days after Rabbi Weil left when Karl's father was elected head himself.

Although Karl had felt uneasy when he visited the other Hartlands he had now lost about the only person who would play with him. His schoolfriends had never been very close and only Rudolph had been prepared to come home. Now even he had become evasive. 'We are very busy and my mother says I can't go out all the time,' he said uneasily. Another boy who lived round the corner was more explicit. 'My father says I am not to go into a Jew's house.'

So Karl went for long walks with the dog or he went across to the park. He had a season ticket and he drifted in and out as he wanted to. He went to exhibitions on goat-keeping, on African flora, and on German racial purity. They were showing a film in the exhibition hall and he went in. It was a film about mental handicap – or degeneration as they called it. All sorts of handicaps were shown and they were photographed in such a way as to be utterly repulsive. The strident voice went on and on. 'And the largest group contributing to the number of degenerates is, of course, the Jews.' Then they showed a Jewish girl jabbering incoherently. The question was asked rhetorically: 'Are we to tolerate people like that? How much longer must we pay the price for degeneracy?'

There was a small zoo for children and Karl fed biscuits to dwarf goats. He ate quantities of sausage from stalls and generally drifted around. Now that he had a camera to take pictures of anything he liked, he photographed flowers, his grandfather, and the dog – and he was very lonely. He disappeared into the cellar more often.

The cellar was huge. There was the boiler room and the coke store and in the middle was now a store of furniture. When Grandfather and Grandmother Freudenberg moved into the house their furniture, or at least all the 'good' furniture was stored in the cellar under huge grey dust sheets. Karl crawled underneath and somewhere in the middle he was able to hollow out a den for himself. All he had to do was to move some chairs and push a table forward and he had a little room that no one knew of. He found a clay model from which a plaster mould and then a bronze head of Grandfather Freudenberg had been cast. It was the same size as his real head and painted green. The eyes stared horribly. Karl decided to make the head a target for his air gun. He placed it behind a chair and he shot it. With each shot a bit of clay split off and he painted each hole with red poster paint and imagined he was executing the old man. He would cry and groan as if he had been hit and would stagger to the head and paint it. He would light a stub of candle and make a store of his money and provisions in case of capture. In one of the novels he was reading the hero always carried a set of tools to effect an escape from impossible situations, and Karl thought he needed similar equipment. He bought himself a set of tiny screwdrivers. a miniature torch and, of course, installed his guns. He put everything in one of the cupboards of a huge Chippendale type sideboard. In another part of the cellar was the wine store; there were a number of wooden bottle holders and each one was locked. Sometimes there were deliveries of wine and Karl helped his father to store the bottles, and his father told him where they had come from and how the wine was grown. Mostly the wines were white from the Rhine and Moselle, and they were usually drunk by themselves after supper, rather than with the meal. Visitors were often given fruit, biscuits and wine in the evening. Karl had discovered that if he put a bottle of wine into the large boiler it would explode and a huge sheet of blue flame would shoot out as the glass cracked and the alcohol burned. He would shoot at empty bottles and smash them with pieces of coke.

Chapter 7

On the wireless it said that a Jewish lad had shot and seriously wounded a German embassy official in Paris. 'If he dies there will be serious trouble,' said Father, 'it would be best if you did not go to school tomorrow morning.' Very early in the morning there was a telephone call. 'They have set fire to the synagogue and they are arresting everybody. We must get out of the house,' Karl's father said and he told the maids to go to their homes. Then as an afterthought: 'The dog can't stay here by himself.' So Karl took the dog to the Rademachers and they said they would be pleased to look after him. Grandfather Freudenberg thought he would like to stay in the house just in case anyone called. Karl was impressed with the way his father stayed so calm. He seemed to know exactly what should be done. They walked down the main road and no one seemed to notice them. The synagogue was about two miles away and they walked at a leisurely pace. They stopped for coffee and a cake on the way. 'We might as well have a leisurely day,' said his father. He walked hand in hand with Karl, and Karl wanted to know why it was all going so badly for Jews. 'I can't really understand it myself,' said his father. 'We have not done this country any harm, and now they treat us as if we were enemies. In the past the government favoured the Jews and Jews were protected by the king from anti-semitism. Now the government has turned against us. I think there is real danger of war. Hitler seems to be provoking everyone, and when I listen to Radio Luxembourg I can tell that everyone in Europe is turning against Germany.'

Karl asked if they should get out of the country. 'I think you and Margot should go. I can't. There is the Jewish community to look after, and the bank. Grandfather Freudenberg can't be left and he is too old to start another life somewhere else.'

As they came near the synagogue Father said, 'Let's keep in the background in case someone recognises us,' and they walked on. There were clusters of people just standing about and watching. The front gate was closed and smoke was coming out of the roof. 'It is all burnt out inside,' Father observed, 'but the building has stood up. It is a very good, solid construction.' Smoke came out of the top windows and the windows in the rooms where Karl had had his religious instruction lessons were broken. There was no sign of the fire brigade and a small group of storm troopers stood there looking as if all this had nothing to do with them.

'I suppose all our books and prayer shawls are burnt,' said Karl.

'That's the least of our problems now the official in Paris is dead,' said his father. 'Let's go and see what's happening in Lindenstrasse.' That was the street in which the bank was.

The flat in which Grandmother Hartland used to live was now occupied by his father's senior assistant, Mr Mond. He was a huge man and Father was very fond of him. 'We have always worked together and I know I can trust him absolutely. The advantage is that he is not a Jew so he can give us a bit of protection. They won't harm a non-Jewish family.' When Mr Mond married, Karl's mother had reached into the glass cabinet and had taken out a Copenhagen parrot for his wedding present. Mrs Mond had come to say thank you for the splendid present, and Karl was a bit puzzled that she should be so pleased when Mutti had only taken it out of the glass case which had so many other figures in it. The families did not visit each other and relations were formal, but Father said he would be lost without Mr Mond.

They went up the stairs. The bank was to the left. There was a huge oak counter where people brought in their day's takings; behind that were high desks for the clerks. They all sat on high chairs and carried enormous ledgers about. Everything was either brown or green and very solid. There were two safes, one of which stood in the front room, and another huge one in the back into which one could walk and its door had several locks.

Father told Karl that during the Spartacist rising men had come into the bank with hand grenades; they had asked Mr Mond for the key, and when he said he had not got it they went out again. 'They might have shot him. They shot a lot of other people. There was a dead man lying in the gutter. Your mother was in the cellar and she was carrying Margot at the time. We did not want her to be upset and so we did not tell her about it; we had to stay in the cellar for days.' He had showed Karl the bullet marks on the wall outside. The bank belonging to the other Hartlands was further down the road, and the huge columns outside also had the little pitted holes in them.

In the bank there was a further room behind the counter and that room was Father's. It had a huge desk, and on it stood a porcelain vase with holes in the sides and water at the bottom. A candle inside it was lit. 'That's to disperse cigar smoke,' Father explained. Karl rarely saw him without a cigar in his mouth. He smoked two sorts, big ones after meals or when there was a special occasion, and little square ones all the time. For a change he would take out a pipe and smoke sweet Dutch tobacco. Karl had started to smoke cigarettes, but Margot teased him. 'You smoke like a lady, funny little puffs. Inhale deeply,' and that Karl could not do. In Father's room there was also a special fireplace. It was made with porcelain tiles and came from Holland. It was green and there were little turrets on it. Behind Father's room was the conference room and it had a huge table covered with a green baize cloth. The walls were lined with wood, and behind the panelling were cupboards full of old files.

Whenever Karl came into the bank everyone was very friendly to him, and asked him how school was and what he was going to do; but really people were busy and he knew that he was disturbing them. To keep him amused Father gave him wads of inflation money. The inflation had happened a long time ago and the price of everything had risen astronomically. 'You couldn't get a bus ticket for a million marks,' Father said. When people were paid they rushed out and bought bread and other food because if they waited they would not have been able to pay, as prices rose every day. A man could not even carry his wages away in a suitcase, it took so much paper. As a reminder of those terrible days trays of the old money were kept in a cardboard box and Karl used the notes for playing bank robbers.

Father talked to Mr Mond and they decided to take the plaque outside down. 'They might give us a miss if they can't see the name,' Mr Mond said. So they went out and took the brass plate down. It said Levi Hartland and Sons. It was brightly polished brass and the letters were slightly worn because they had been rubbed by the cleaners so many times. Neither Father nor Mr Mond found it easy to get the brass plate off. They were not used to doing jobs like that, but succeeded after a struggle. It had been there more than a hundred years, said Father as they looked at the stone that was unplastered because it had been covered by the plaque before. Mr Mond told Father that he had rung all the staff and told them not to come, and he also warned Father that they were picking up Jewish men from their homes.

Karl and Father walked back towards their home. There were more people than usual in the streets and occasionally they could hear the klaxons of police cars. They passed a shop that had been smashed and all the shoes from the window scattered over the pavement together with plate glass. 'That was Wallach's shop,' said Father, 'he is one of our customers.' A woman and a man stepped over the glass carrying boxes out of the shop.

'I think I will have to disappear for the night,' said Father. 'I'll sleep in the secret place in the loft.' Karl did not know about any secret place. He thought he knew the house inside out, but he had no idea where his father could mean.

'It's inside the roof,' said Father. 'It is like a double roof. You push the woodwork back and there is a space: enough space for a bed. You and I are the only people who know about this and no one else must know.'

Karl felt he was being sworn to secrecy and he agreed not to

118

talk about it. Father said he would put a mattress up there and Karl was not even to tell Grandfather Freudenberg that he was in the house. 'If anyone asks say I have gone for a trip. And don't use the phone, they might be listening in.'

Karl remembered one frightening afternoon not so long ago when in the middle of an afternoon conversation while they were having coffee and cakes, Mrs Neumann had jumped up and rushed over to the telephone and hit it with a cushion, and then tried to cover it up. She shouted, 'They can listen through the telephone, the bastards, they are everywhere and they try to listen.' Karl thought it was quite funny as he hated Mrs Neumann. She had a huge bosom, a bit like a cathedral – if one stone or wire was removed one feared the lot would come down. She always looked angry and discontented and even the dead fox skin that she wore round her neck seemed to be rearing up as if it might bite at any moment.

Karl helped his father to drag the mattress up to the loft and for the first time he saw the secret place. What looked like ordinary deep brown pine board was in fact a door, and there was quite a space behind it. Once the 'door' was closed it was impossible to spot because the light up there was not all that good. The loft was used for drying washed linen if it was wet outside, and there were clothes lines all over the place. In the corner on the opposite side were trunks full of the books they had bought out of Grandmother Hartland's flat when she died. Karl occasionally went up to the loft to roller skate, but he preferred his cave in the cellar and so the roof had not received much attention from him. Father brought some candles and matches and later on went into hiding. Grandfather was in the drawing room reading the paper and if he was aware of what was going on he did not talk to Karl about it. He just said, 'Your father has gone away, has he?'

The doorbell rang. Karl went to the door and opened it to two policemen in civilian clothes. They had come to collect any arms there might be in the house. Karl said, 'There is only my air gun and the toy guns.'

'We will take those,' they said. 'One never knows.' And they took Karl's new air gun and the broken one and his starter pistol. Karl did not tell them about the other gun in his cave. It was an imitation six shooter and he could not bring himself to mention it.

They gave Karl a long look. 'Where is your father?'

'He has gone away.'

They seemed satisfied with that reply and went back to the car that was waiting outside. Karl was shaking with fear. What if his father had been at home to them? Would they have arrested him? The phone rang, it was Ella to ask how things were going and Karl said it was all right. 'Did you hear that they have burnt down the Michaels' house?' They were the owners of a store and the house was not very far away. Karl did not know what he should do and just put the receiver down because his father had warned him not to talk on the phone. It rang again, this time it was Margot from Berlin. Karl hated all this phoning and tried to be brief. 'How are things. Where is Father?' In accordance with instructions, Karl said, 'Father has gone away,' not realising that 'gone away' meant that he had been arrested in the language of the time and so Margot was in a state of complete panic. She shouted at Karl to tell her more and he said there was nothing to tell and hung up the phone. He did not go to bed but went to sleep on the couch in the living room with his clothes on.

He was fast asleep when the front doorbell rang. Not the usual ring but long, long rings that just went on. Karl jumped up and rushed downstairs. There was also a crashing sound from the back door. A group of storm troopers pushed their way in.

'You the only one here?'

'No, there is also my grandfather.'

Grandfather Freudenberg appeared on the stairs. He too was fully dressed.

'Any weapons in the house?' they asked.

'We handed the air gun to the police,' Karl said.

He was thinking, what if they set the house on fire. Father is in the attic. If I tell them he is there they will kill him. The men were in brown uniforms and carried pistols and daggers. Their gun holsters, Karl noticed, were open. Karl heard a crashing sound from the kitchen. The men charged right up the stairs at great speed, a bit like Karl when he was pretending to be engaged in house-to-house fighting. There were crashes and bangs all over the place. An officer came up to Karl. 'Show us round.' Karl used very polite language and behaved like a guide in a country house. 'This is the drawing room.' He saw to his horror that the men were turning out drawers. They just pulled them out, turned them over and everything fell on the floor. The book cupboard went over.

'We are looking for arms,' the officer explained. 'Where is the dog?' he went on, looking at the lead hanging from a hook in the dressing room.'

'He has been sent away, honoured, sir,' Grandfather said. He followed the men at a respectful distance.

There were crashes in the kitchen and noises in the dining room, but Karl followed the officer. 'This is the bedroom of my parents.' One of the men went up to a chest of drawers and pulled it open and cases of bandages and plasters fell out. 'Look at what these Jews have got,' the storm trooper said. 'They wallow in everything and we have got nothing.' They rushed from room to room. Karl saw one trooper with his camera. That was too much. 'That's my camera,' he shouted, 'you are stealing my camera.' The trooper turned on him and took his shirt and twisted it round so that it was tight round Karl's throat. 'Listen, Jew boy, the storm troopers don't steal.' Karl's knees went weak and there was nothing he could do. The man let him go, pushing him away. He had a round face and glittering eyes and Karl saw the embroidered numbers on the flashes very closely. He stomped away and Karl followed.

He saw his camera at the top of the stairs, it had been stepped on and the lens had been pushed right in. He began to cry quietly. He heard his grandfather explaining to the man who had complained about the number of bandages. 'You see, your honour, this is usually a big household. Would you like some wine, your honour?' Karl hated his grandfather, he was crawling like a caricature of a ghetto Jew. Why didn't he stand up to them?

He stood with tears running down his face and again thought that they might set the house on fire. 'Are you going to burn the house?' he asked the officer.

'I don't think so,' he said, and Karl did not feel reassured.

Men were trooping down the stairs. 'Been right up to the top?' the officer asked. 'Let's go.'

One man came up with a meat cleaver. 'Look what I've found.'

Karl said, 'But that comes from the kitchen, that is for the kitchen.'

'You can't tell,' said the officer. 'You could kill someone with that, it could be a weapon.'

Karl felt he was being tried and found guilty. 'Please sir,' he begged, 'please don't burn the house.'

'We'll let you off this time,' said the officer. 'Come on everybody, we have got lots of work to do.' And they all went out.

Grandfather rang the police and said, 'Please come. The house has been attacked!' The police said there was nothing they could do but they might send someone along later. In the meantime the bell rang again and this time a group of SS men came in.

'So they have been here before us,' one of them said. 'We are supposed to protect this house. We don't want it destroyed. We want to be able to use these good houses. Got anything to drink?'

Karl felt he had found a friend in all his troubles and he rushed downstairs to find his father's best brandy. He offered round cigars as well and the man seemed contented. He was not very old, perhaps twenty, and he was not at ease. Karl brought him his camera. 'Look what happened to my camera.' He could not add that it was his best barmitzvah present. He did not think Jewish matters were appropriate at that point.

The SS man looked at the camera. 'Perhaps it can be mended,' he said.

Karl looked at the camera closely. 'Perhaps it can, but it will be an expensive job.'

'Where is your father?' the man asked.

'He has gone away.'

'Has he gone abroad?'

'I don't know.'

'You are right not to tell me; I expect he has gone abroad. That's the only place for you people; there is nothing for you here any more.'

The doorbell rang and a policeman appeared The SS man said, 'Will you guard this place? There is only this boy and an old man. We have searched the house and there aren't any arms here.'

Karl thought to himself, 'If they find my gun they will burn the house down.' But the SS men left, one of them carrying Father's brandy bottle. The policeman looked at the drawing room. 'They have made a mess.' Karl and he went round the house. Every room had been turned inside out. In the living room Karl noticed that someone had drawn a dagger right across the painting that hung over the sofa. It looked strange – the black streaks right across what had been a ploughman working on his field. More canvases had been slashed in other rooms and a lot of crockery had been broken. A flower vase had been smashed into the bath tub. In the dining room the Spode tea set was all over the place, not all of it broken. It was very old and had belonged to Grandmother Hartland and Karl liked the flower patterns on it. He picked up the pieces that were still whole and started to tidy them up.

'Go to bed boy,' said his grandfather, 'we will tidy up tomorrow.'

The doorbell rang again and it was one of the SS men. 'I wonder if you have anything left to drink?'

'Certainly, Mr SS man,' said Grandfather.

The man sat at the table and poured out some Moselle for himself. 'We have been on duty since early morning, it's been a rough day,' he said.

'I can understand that, Mr SS man. It has been a hard day for you. It must be difficult. Would you, perhaps ...' (here Grandfather slipped him a bundle of notes) ... 'if perhaps you and your gentlemen colleagues would like to have a drink?'

Grandfather knew how to deal with the enemy. He was hundreds of years back, in the Middle Ages, buying off a pogrom, and the SS man liked his humility.

'Thanks, I'll go and see my girl friend now.'

'That's right, Mr SS man, you enjoy yourself, have a good time.'

The man went out, clutching a second bottle of wine that Grandfather had pressed on him. He had obviously liked Grandfather and his visit.

Grandfather said, 'It is better to have people like that friendly. Go to bed boy.'

Karl went upstairs and saw his father coming down. 'Are they gone?'

'Yes.'

'I'll go and have a look at the police station and see if they are still arresting people. They may have finished by now.'

Father had a huge black smudge across his face and cobwebs in his hair and Karl started to laugh, he looked so ridiculous and Karl had never seen his father look so dirty. He went to bed, and when he woke up his father was there and he said: 'They have stopped, but I think we'd better be out of the way for the day.'

They left Grandfather alone in the house. Father thought he would be safe because he was far too old to be any trouble. He had looked over the house at the mess. 'They are barbarians. They have smashed wine bottles instead of opening them properly, just to get a drink. What a bunch of criminals. And they have slashed some of the pictures. You can tell they are an ignorant bunch; they have only damaged the really bad pictures. And why did they stamp on your camera? They really are the end.'

They went to a phone booth and father phoned Mr Mond. 'They have been in the bank as well,' he told Karl when he came out, 'and they made a terrible mess of the place. But we fooled them, we put out-of-date files in the front room and they threw them all over the place and the important ones haven't been touched.' Father saw this as a victory. 'They are fools as well as savages,' he added. 'Let's go down to the bank and have a look.'

Mr Mond let them in and it was an incredible mess. Type-writers had been thrown against walls, desks turned over, stools smashed to bits and the safe that stood in the room had been turned over. The big safe had marks on it but they had not been able to get it open. The stove in Father's room was smashed but the conference room in the back was untouched; the Monds' flat had not been raided either. Aryans were exempt even if they worked for Jews.

'We will get this cleared up in no time,' said Mr Mond.

But Father said, 'We will just have to finish everything off now and close down. They won't let us go on. We survived the war, the Spartacists, inflation, the depression and now they have ruined everything. What a pity.'

Karl thought his father sounded very calm. 'We'll disappear for the rest of the day,' he told Mr Mond. 'Find out if they are still arresting people. They had stopped when I had a look yesterday.'

'You mean you went to the police station and had a look?' Mr Mond sounded really amazed.

'Yes, I thought that was the one place where they would not look for me, and when they were arresting people, one car after another came in and the whole place was in an uproar, lights on, and shouting, so you could tell what was going on. I wonder what happens to the people they have taken in.'

'They call it protective custody,' said Mr Mond bitterly, 'but they only seem to take young men, people up to fifty or so. They called for you here as well, but I think they had to fill some sort of quota and when they had a certain number they stopped.'

Karl went to the station with his father and they took a train to Düsseldorf. It wasn't all that far away and Father was fond of the town. 'I'll tell you what we will do. First we'll have a really slap-up breakfast, like the ones I used to have in England : ham and eggs, and rolls; and then we'll go for a walk and then we'll have lunch and then we'll go to a cimema. How about that?'

Karl was in raptures. This was his idea of a good day. Their ham and eggs came in a little metal dish. The ham had been cooked in butter and the egg on top of it had been baked rather than fried, but it had a gorgeous smell and they both had a lot of strong coffee as well. They looked at the shops, ate cakes and walked round parks. There seemed less evidence of wrecked shops in the town.

'It's more of an international town, and they don't want foreigners to know what is going on. It is much worse in the small country districts than in Essen. They really let themselves go. You know this is a dreadful time. I am only glad about one thing, and that is that your poor mother did not have to go through it all.'

Karl wondered how his mother would have coped and thought that the idea of his father in the secret loft and the SS looking for arms below was not right for her. She was an odd mixture. In an emergency she was calm, but she could be timid and easily frightened as well. Karl was glowing in the knowledge that he had coped. He forgot about crying when they had broken his camera and he had been threatened by the SA man.

They had a good lunch, small pieces of fillet steak and fried potatoes, and his father had wine; then tart and more coffee. Then they walked about, 'to get our appetite back' said Father, and they saw a film. Karl loved the cinema, and as far as he was concerned there was no such thing as a bad film. It was a good day for him. They saw the *Lives of the Bengal Lancers*.

Suddenly Karl remembered the gun he had hidden in the furniture caves in the house. 'I'll dig a hole in the garden,' he said to himself, 'and I'll put it in and the sods will never find it.' That was his little victory, like his father and the files. After the film there was a variety show and Karl was enthralled by the tap dancer who danced to the tune of 'The Lambeth Walk'. For weeks afterwards Karl 'tap danced', making a terrible mess on the linoleum.

After a light supper of sausage, ham, rolls and potato salad they went back to Essen by train. Father had bought some papers – there were going to be more serious reprisals against the Jewish communities. A fine of millions of marks was to be imposed and further measures would be announced.

Every morning now Karl would rush for the paper and see what the next measure against the Jews was going to be. Then one day it said: 'No Aryan German child will in future risk being contaminated by having to sit next to a Jew in school.' That was it. Karl felt an enormous sense of relief. He would not have to go back to school. His father was more worried.

'We must get you an education. You can't stop at this point, I must get you into a school.' Karl was happy as he was. The house was cleared up. There had been a lot of broken glass but no more serious damage. His camera, they said, could not be repaired. It was not worth it, the man in the camera shop said. 'How did you get it into that state?' 'Stepped on it,' Karl answered.

A lady stopped him in the street. 'We saw it, we saw it all,' she said excitedly. 'We looked out of our back window, and my husband had the binoculars out and we saw them smashing everything up.'

Karl said that they had tidied everything up now and all was in order again and she said that she was glad to hear it.

Grandfather Freudenberg came home from his shopping expedition, looking very fed up. 'They won't serve us in the greengrocer's any more. They said they were sorry, but someone had been to see them from the Party and told them they must not serve Jews any more.'

Karl said, 'We will just go somewhere they don't know us. I don't look Jewish and they will serve me.' And from then onwards he did that sort of shopping. Grandfather did not like going out of the house any more.

As Karl was no longer able to go back to school, they wrote saying would he please collect his final report. Karl went uneasily. He was no longer sure how he would be received and he went to the principal's office. He said to the secretary, 'I have come to collect my report,' and she leaned round the door and shouted to the director of the school, 'One of the Jewish boys is here. He wants his certificate.'

'Oh send him in.' Karl had not even seen the director, let alone talked to him, since the interview before admission to the gymnasium.

'So, you are leaving us,' he said.

Karl thought to himself: 'No, you are throwing me out,' but did not dare to do anything but say 'yes' and ask if he could have the report, please. The director asked Karl what he was going to do, and Karl muttered that he was thinking of going to England or possibly America.

'Well, goodbye and good luck.' He shook Karl by the hand and Karl clicked his heels and bowed forward smartly.

'Go and say goodbye to your form master,' he added, 'I think you should say goodbye.'

Karl crept up to the staff room. He had never been inside it: no child in the school had ever been in there. He knocked on the door, and when it was opened the air was thick with cigar smoke and the teachers were standing in groups talking.

'I'll get Mr Fleck for you,' one of them said.

When he emerged, Karl spoke: 'I was told to say goodbye to you. I am leaving.'

'Ah, yes, well what are you going to do?'

Karl said he thought they might emigrate to England or America.

'Yes, that's a good idea, I expect all your money is over there by now. You seem to have international connections everywhere.'

Karl said he didn't know about their money.

'I don't expect you to tell me about that,' Mr Fleck replied, as if he knew a secret. 'Goodbye, then.'

Karl thought to himself, 'You big arsehole,' nodded his head, said goodbye and went out of the building with a sense of relief.

The report said 'adequate performance' on every subject and underneath it just had 'precocious'. Karl showed the report to his father who commented: 'I suppose they were afraid they would be in trouble if they praised anything you had done.'

Karl thought to himself that if anything, the report was rather kind to him, considering how little homework he had done.

At home the dog had been brought back and one afternoon Karl tried to repair the slashed painting of the ploughman. He found his mother's oil paints in a box room and glued paper to the back of the picture. Then he matched the greens and browns and when his father came home showed him what he had done. His father was pleased. 'Let's hang it up again,' he said. 'It is as good as it ever was, you are clever.'

Every day there were new laws and Karl took the paper upstairs in the morning to see what the next one was. First there was the fine: every Jew had to give up a quarter of the value of his property to pay for the crime of the assassination; then no Jew was allowed to go to a cinema any more; no Jew was allowed to own either silver or gold. 'They want to take everything away from us. I really must get you and Margot out of the country,' said his father.

For Karl the rule about the cinemas was the worst. He had taken money from his father's pocket again, but when he looked at the note in the lavatory after the raid he saw to his horror that he had taken a hundred marks. His normal haul was five or ten. A hundred was completely outside his scope. He did not know what to do. He thought he could not put it back. That, he convinced himself, took longer than taking it out. So Karl decided to use the money.

He was surprised how easy it was to have it changed. 'Can you change this for my daddy,' he said at the post office and they gave him ten mark notes and Karl felt much relieved; that was much more the sort of money he could handle. It was easier for him to do what he wanted to do now that he was not going to school any more. 'Don't get into lazy habits,' said his father. 'Learn English and do some mathematics while I am away.'

Karl opened the books occasionally but could not really concentrate. He thought about his gun which he had buried at the bottom of the garden. He had taken it to pieces and had dug a separate hole for each part, he would dig one up occasionally to see how it was surviving in the soil. 'One day I'll come back and dig up the parts and assemble the gun again,' he said to himself.

With the money he began to buy toys, he went to the main toyshop in the town, a paradise. There were three floors and the most beautiful soldiers, but Karl was now interested in battleships. The models were in scale and beautifully made and expensive. 'Here you are, sir,' said the lady, and handed Karl the parcel. He was a good customer.

He went back home with the fleet and put the parcel at the cellar door, as he always did with contraband, and then he rang at the front door where Ella let him in.

'Where have you been?'

'Shopping.'

'I don't see any shopping,' she said.

'That is because I did not find what I wanted,' Karl replied.

The ships were smuggled into his room and hidden. He played with them in the mornings. The blue lino was the ocean and he fought the battle of the cruiser *Emden* which operated in the Pacific and was finally destroyed by a great fleet. He had seen a film about that.

For his films he decided to be very cunning; if they would not allow him into cinemas in Essen he would go somewhere else. In the afternoons he took a train to a neighbouring town and went there. He was always scared. What if suddenly streams of police and SS men came in and checked everyone's identity? What if someone recognised him? In the intervals, which Karl came to hate, he sank very low in his seat and pulled up his collar and hoped the lights would go out quickly. He would leave the cinema through the emergency exit and come out in side streets. He saw *David Copperfield* and wept over his fate and he loved Shirley Temple. He bought a film magazine every week and he learned that numbers of films were banned in Germany because they were either made by Jews or were in themselves corrupting.

One evening he felt desperately ill. His breathing hurt him and he only wanted to lie down. As he had pretended to be ill so many times, Karl almost did not believe in his good fortune when he found that he really was ill. He tested the pain in his chest tenderly; he wasn't imagining it. His father told him to go to bed and Dr Levi was called and diagnosed pleurisy. Karl was put into his mother's bed so that everyone looking after him would not have to climb to the top of the house. It was a huge soft bed. Sophy said appreciatively, 'I bet they had a good bounce in that bed.' Karl lay back and was happy to be ill. He did not even have to heat the thermometer. His body produced all the heat needed to keep everyone attentive and kind to him. The dog was exiled to the balcony and Karl could hear his anguished howls. He heard people talk and food went past to his corner of the world. When Karl had been left a tray of tempting food ('The boy isn't eating properly'), he would sneak out and throw Pisser a veal cutlet or some pieces of sausage. That was when the love between the two was more deeply bonded. When Karl really begged, the dog was allowed in for a brief visit, but he was so overjoyed then that he forgot his training and just raced round the room, yelping and jumping up on the bed to lick Karl.

Dr Levi came every day. He listened to Karl's breathing and they talked about emigration. 'We must all get out. They don't want us here and now they have arrested so many people, what will happen?' The men who had been arrested gradually drifted back home away from what the authorities called 'protective custody'. It was explained on the wireless that the government feared that the population was infuriated with the Jews, that they would rise up and kill them all, and so, for their own good, they had been taken in.

The gardener's son, who was Ella's boy friend, was sitting in the kitchen. He told Karl that he had been in Dachau for six weeks and now he had been released on condition that he leave the country within three days. He was very sunburnt and his hair had been shorn. It was as short as Grandfather Freudenberg's. Karl asked him what it had been like and he said he had signed a document which said that if he talked to anyone about Dachau he would be re-arrested. To console him Karl said, 'Anyhow you look nice and sunburnt,' and the boy thought that was very funny. He talked about going to Hong Kong. Visas could be bought and there might be work for him there as a lorry driver.

Karl gradually got better, but he stayed in the bed next to his father and just went to his room upstairs to play or to smoke his cigarettes. He smoked them leaning out of the window and he thought it odd that his father, who never stopped smoking himself, did not like it when Karl came in reeking of tobacco. Karl smoked Abdullah cigarettes. They came in tin boxes and had a picture of a pyramid and a camel on the outside.

Many stories were told about the raids. Not only synagogues had been burnt, but in a small village along the Rhine a Jewish couple had been tied together and thrown into the water. In other parts of Essen men and boys were beaten up when the storm troopers came into their houses. It seemed to have happened when people protested or tried to keep the intruders out. Karl was never told these things directly. He listened while people talked and sometimes they stopped when he was around. This made him cross because he realised that they did not want to upset him and were not treating him as a grown-up.

He went to cinemas nearly every day now, or to a fairground which had been set up behind the station. Here he could shoot air guns, and ones with caps, and he won prizes; paper flowers and figures made from plaster. What he really wanted was a huge teddy bear but his shooting scores never reached those heights. He saw the fattest lady in the world, an immense sad looking lady dressed in satin which bulged out at every point. She sat there knitting, which was a bit disappointing.

He saw the two-headed foetus in an immense glass bottle, and what struck him was the greyness and the way the little arms were folded over each other. He drifted from one thing to another, but he liked the way the show people treated him with courtesy. Here he was not just an outcast but a big spender who shot guns and he was welcome.

In the evening Karl's father would listen to the news on Radio Luxembourg. He told Karl that the news on the German radio was not truthful, so they listened to the broadcasts in German from Luxembourg which described the raids in November. The German radio just spoke of the penal measures and the iniquities they were punishing rather than of the many people who had been arrested, the homes smashed and people killed. Father asked Karl and his cousin Joseph to take the silver things to the town pawnshop, and explained they would only be paid for the weight of the metal, not for the value of each article. Father also said that the price set for the silver was pretty poor. 'We must obey the law, though. If we don't they will only do something worse to us.' So all the silver was collected together. It was first put on the floor in the dining room with the cutlery. It was heavy stuff, all curly and baroque. Each piece had Mutti's initials on it. Then there was the tea set. It had always stood on the sideboard in the dining room. There was another silver coffee pot and many other things which had been part of Karl's world. They were allowed to keep one place setting of silver for each member of the family and that was all. The things were bundled together and put into two suitcases. Karl, remembering the unpleasant episode with his mother's suitcase, demanded that they should be allowed a taxi and his father agreed. At the municipal pawnshop they sat with everyone else pawning their things and it seemed a sad place to Karl. Next to him was a woman with a pile of sheets, and other people just had one thing like a wireless or a piece of carpet. Everything they had brought was listed carefully and weighed and then they were paid with a large wad of bank notes. The only problem with Karl's things seemed to be the pearls; they had belonged to Grandmother Freudenberg and Mutti and they did not seem to know whether they were real pearls or cultured ones. 'They are a bunch of fools,' commented Karl's father, 'and they have just made robbery look legal.'

Chapter 8

Very early one morning the doorbell rang. Karl was half asleep but heard his father get up, and then some talk, and steps, and some banging. Then he went to sleep again. In the morning his father said, 'They have taken Sophy away; they said they are arresting all Polish Jews, and they are going to be sent back to Poland. She was only allowed to take a small suitcase.'

Karl was staggered; it had all happened just like that and now Sophy was gone. When Ella was downstairs in the kitchen he went back upstairs and looked into the girl's bedroom. It was obvious that Sophy did not have time to pack and had just grabbed a few things. The door of the wardrobe was wide open and her black and pink dress was hanging there. She had only bought it a few days before and had shown it to Karl in the kitchen and he had liked it. Ella had been less kind to Sophy when she saw the dress, and muttered that she would get some nasty disease if she carried on the way she was going. 'What disease?' asked Karl. 'Just you watch out,' said Ella, and it was obvious that Sophy was furious with her for saying a thing like that; Karl was interested to see two people quarrel in that way. Now he looked at the wardrobe and remembered how he had chased Sophy when she was half-naked, and he felt sorry that she was gone.

That evening in the paper there was a photograph of a great column of people being marched towards the railway station. Karl looked for Sophy in the picture but could not find her. 'There are the Lesers,' said his father. Mrs Leser had taught in the Jewish elementary school and there she was carrying things in a blanket or a sheet over her shoulder. She was wearing heavy walking shoes and her husband was carrying a rucksack. Later, stories came back that they had been taken to the frontier and told to walk over to the Polish side, but that the Poles had refused to let them in and they had been left to rot in no-man's-land. Just a few – who had relatives who were prepared to look after them – were allowed in, but many perished of exposure. The *Essen Gazette* had a caption under the photograph which said, 'At last Essen is being cleaned up'.

At the Jewish community office there were long queues of people who wanted to emigrate and who needed help. Each family was given a number, and they tried to find them places abroad but it was not easy: in Palestine there was a quota; in England it was difficult without a special permit and a guarantor – someone had to say they would be prepared to look after the refugee, be responsible for his good behaviour, and put sums of money aside as a guarantee that they would stand surety for any debt or expenses. In the United States there was a quota system; only a certain number of any one ethnic group would be allowed in. Applicants would be given numbers and when their number came up they could leave. Karl became an expert in all this because the people round him talked about little else. It was easier for people with money to leave than for people who were poor, and it was better still if you had relatives in a particular country. Most of the Hartland acquaintances and friends tried several countries and just hoped that one would come up. Karl's father told him that he was trying to get him to England with a whole group of students and that he could go to school there. A former director of a Jewish school was collecting a group of likely boys, and fees and expenses were to be paid from home. The problem was that the German authorities would only allow tiny amounts of German money to be taken out of the country and it was illegal to own any foreign currency. So it was only those who had smuggled money out illegally who could expect to live from their own income.

Karl's father pointed out that most of the people who were stuck were those with professions they could not practise anywhere else. For instance, what was Mr Kugel, a lawyer, going to do? He did not know either the language or the law of any other country and he had no certificates of competence anyone else would accept. The same was true of a banker or even a doctor. A doctor might be allowed to practise if he passed the examinations of his new country, but until then he would have to rely on charity or work at something else, like cousin Joseph who was training to be a waiter or a butler instead of going into the bank. Karl thought it was hilarious when Joseph elegantly served the supper with two silver spoons in one hand, deftly holding a potato between them until it ended up on the plate.

'I'm going into the Foreign Legion,' said Karl, 'that's what I will do if all else fails.' He had just seen a film about the Foreign Legion and it said that it was the final destiny of the lonely and the unhappy; he saw himself in a desert fort firing at the Bedouins. They all laughed and said, 'Bravo, don't let them get you down. That's one thing about Karl, he is bound to get on.'

They met the cantor in the street. Since he had instructed Karl in the mysteries of reading the holy scriptures they had not met. As with everyone now the first question asked was, 'Where are you going?' Karl immediately translated what were really rather vague plans into definite fact. 'I'm going to England.' 'Ah, England, well you look like a typical little Englishman already, all you need is a pipe.'

Although Karl didn't know what a typical Englishman was supposed to look like, the thought pleased him and he saw himself with a pipe in his mouth, plus-fours and a flat cap. Plusfours he wore already, they were what young boys wore when they had grown out of short trousers. It was the first outward sign of being more of an adult. Had he stayed on at school his teachers would by now be addressing him with the more formal 'you' instead of 'thou'.

Hats were a sore point between Karl and his father. One day Karl's father told him that he should wear a proper hat, and handed him a thing with a brim which Karl immediately hated.

'You must wear a hat,' his father said, 'to be properly dressed. Come on, try this one.'

Karl had loved his school cap because it was a nice blue colour and had a military look about it – like the cavalry in the wars against Napoleon, he thought. But this was a dreary hat. He seemed to disappear under it. But he obeyed, and wore it to the town registry office to get his birth certificate. He stood in a long line patiently and when his turn came the official looked up and snapped, 'Hat off, you are not in a synagogue now.' Karl blushed a deep shade of red and tore his hat off.

More plans were made. Margot could go to England as a maid servant. Her future employer was to be the guarantor and this seemed an easy way to get permission to enter the country. Before long a letter came from a small place in Sussex and Margot's future employer, a Mrs Prudence Barratt, wrote to her. The letter was on thick, bluish paper and the address was printed on it. 'Ah, yes,' said Father, 'they are proper people. Look, the address is embossed on the paper, not just printed on it.' Indeed Karl could feel the slightly raised print. He also looked at the fluent and neatly spaced writing. Father impressed both of them by translating the letter. 'She hopes you will be happy with them, and you will have a room with another girl who also comes from Germany. She says her husband is a high ranking officer. This sounds just the right sort of thing.'

So Margot was going to be the first to go. Her suitcases were packed and she was allowed to take some household goods, like sheets, crockery and a carpet. The linen and the other things were packed in wooden crates, and she took a huge trunk which opened out and had a space like a wardrobe on one side and drawers on the other. When the Freudenberg grandparents had gone for their annual 'cure' to Marienbad they had taken one of these monster trunks each. They went for the cure each year to lose weight and, it was said, 'The liver would also be allowed to rest'. Karl understood that the cure consisted of drinking water that made you go to the lavatory often. His father had added that walks were prescribed, and on these walks the lavatories were fairly widely spaced so the patient had to move at a fair pace to make it to the next one without an accident. Anyhow, all the family returned from the 'cure' a few pounds lighter. Father said that Uncle Arnold from the other Hartland family was such a vigorous taker of the waters that he needed two sets of suits: one pre- and one post-Marienbad.

Margot took the best set of tableware. There were blue and gold rims round each plate, and the last time it had seen daylight was during Karl's barmitzvah dinner party. She also took a carpet Karl liked very much. It was the one which he had pulled away from under her feet when she was standing on the other side of the brown velvet curtain.

While the preparations were made for Margot to go, Father told Karl what his own plans were. 'When you leave,' he told him, 'the house will be too big for just Grandfather Freudenberg and me; the girls are planning to leave as well, and so I think I am going to move in with Aunt Cecilia and Aunt Julia. Joseph will be gone by then. His sister is already in America, and there will be plenty of room for us there and we can look after each other.' It took Karl some time to absorb all this news, his world really was falling apart. He just could not understand that anyone could live anywhere else than in the house in which he had grown up. Of course he had not always lived there and remembered the move when he had been very small indeed, something like four years old. He could still see the unpacked suitcase in the room that was to be his until his grandparents moved in. He was holding a wooden bear which his parents had brought him from a holiday in Switzerland.

And now all this was to be ended. He understood that he was going to go to England, but he had thought the house would go on for ever. He knew every smallest detail of it; he had crawled into the rafters, he had crawled along the water pipes to a tank in the roof, all his caves and hiding places were there, his gun was buried in the garden and his cave was in the cellar.

In the meantime he went with his father to Cologne to meet the headmaster of the school he was going to attend in England. He did not take to this man in the very least. He was cross-eyed and talked in a funny way. He began a sentence in a loud voice and ended in a confidential whisper. He spoke only to Karl's father, never to Karl, and everything he said sounded like one spy giving another very secret information. No, he told them, the school did not exist yet, but he was going round Germany collecting promising pupils ('What's promising about me,' thought Karl) and then when he had a good group together they would found the school in England. 'My representative, Mr Selig, is already in England, looking after my interests there.' While Karl hated the headmaster, his father seemed to agree with everything he said and, what was worse, asked what Karl should be doing in the meantime. 'Oh, English, learn a lot of English,' the educationist replied, 'and keep up his geometry, that's important.' He suggested that Karl should be bought a geometry book in English which would be excellent preparation in both fields. On their way home father took him into a bookshop and bought him a fat, green bound volume of Euclidian geometry in English. 'There you are, you can get on with that.' One other thing Karl learnt; he would be found a place in a hostel and would have to wait there until the school could be assembled.

Karl saw that the familiar life he was leading at the moment was deeply threatened. As he was no longer going to school he breakfasted with his father and watched him walk towards the tram stop from the second floor window. When he was safely out of sight he would bring out his drawing materials and try to copy the Mona Lisa. Then he would go to the bookshelves, searching for information about making love, but never found anything very explicit. Love making was still a mystery and no one would really help him. Ella had said if he wanted to know more about screwing he should go to the Stahlstrasse – that's where you paid for it. Karl had money, what remained from the hundred marks, and he decided to make the expedition, but somehow he never got there. Either he went to the toyshop to buy ships or he went to a restaurant or he made an expedition to another town to go to the cinema.

One other possible source of information was an old encyclopaedia, but all he found there was a cross section of the male penis and line drawings of the female genitalia; line drawings and Latin names were not really what he was after. He had tried to talk to Margot, who was nice but vague, and said it would all sort itself out quite naturally and he need not worry about it at present.

At about this time a new law came out that all Jews were to have special identity cards, and they must report to the police station to get them. Karl went on his own. He had never been inside the main police station before. It was a huge building and a policeman stood outside as a guard. He had the usual police uniform on. It was blue, and the helmet was made of a shiny black material. There was a visor and above the visor a circle, a bit like a ventilation funnel on a ship. On the round circle in front of the helmet was a star of silver metal and above the visor a strap which could be tied under the chin. On the belt was a pouch, a leather holster with a revolver in it, and a rubber truncheon. Karl walked past the guard and asked where he should go for his identity card. The man did not even look up from his desk. 'All Jews on the second floor.' Karl went up and saw the endless corridors all painted green, and he could see where the cards were issued because there was a group of people waiting in a line. Karl, mindful of his visit to the registry office, took off his hat as he entered. An index card had to be filled in first. 'Name,' an official snapped at him. And Karl told him his name in the sharp military tone that seemed to be required. 'Karl Lewis Hartland.' (Lewis because of his father's best friend who now lived in Paris and also, conveniently, because it was his dead brother's name as well. 'You have forgotten something,' the official said. 'What about Israel?'

'I'm sorry, Mr Policeman, I had forgotten.'

'You have no right to forget anything,' the man snapped at Karl. 'It is an offence not to add "Israel" to your name. You weren't trying to get away with it and pretend you are not a Yid were you?'

'No, I wasn't, it is just that I haven't got used to the new name yet.'

So they went on – address, date of birth, and Karl produced the birth certificate which he had already fetched from the local registry office.

'Now fingerprints,' the official said. 'Over there,' and Karl went to a table and his prints were taken, first on a card for the file and then on his new identity card which was grey and it folded over. Inside was his photograph which was partly covered by an official stamp. The stamp showed the German eagle clawing a swastika and the swastika was surrounded by a laurel wreath.

Karl's photograph had been taken in a booth. He took two copies to the police station, one for the card and the other for the file, and before he glued it on the official took a long look at him to make sure that it was a likeness. Karl had looked at the photograph for a long time and he hoped it wasn't like him. It showed a podgy child with hair cut very short, wearing a shirt with stripes on it and a silk tie. The photograph only went as far as his shoulders, but he could see he was wearing his sleeveless pullover. Karl would have liked to have thin, sharp features, a brown tan and a strong chin that jutted forward, a wasp-like waist and smart military bearing. On the card it said eyes blue, hair fair, complexion light, and that his name was Karl Lewis *Israel* Hartland. On the front of the card was a huge Gothic letter 'J' which was spread all over the page. There could be no doubt – if Karl ever had to produce that card, everyone would know he was a Jew.

Margot's date for departure was fixed, but before she went Father told her to take Karl and buy him the clothes he would need in England. This was an exciting expedition. The two went off with what was virtually a blank cheque. Remember, Father had said, he can take only one large case and hand baggage and so what you buy must last a long time, because over there he won't have any money of his own. So they went and bought nothing but the best. A gabardine raincoat for autumn, a light cotton raincoat for milder weather, a very heavy overcoat for the winter, and shirts and suits. 'Take away the long trousers,' said Margot 'they only wear plus-fours in England.' So Karl now owned a blue suit and a brown suit and he felt uncomfortable in his very clean, stiff gabardine coat. He had a large brown trunk now, and he was given his mother's suitcase, the one he had dragged home from hospital; he was also going to take a smaller black case he had been given as a present for his barmitzvah.

Soon after the shopping expedition his sister went off to be a servant girl in England. She was dressed in a grey costume, styled in the latest Paris fashion, a little fur was draped round her neck and she carried raw-hide luggage which matched her handbag. The wooden crates full of linen and crockery went later. Before they could go they were inspected by customs officials who drew up lists of everything and gave the value of each article. Father had to pay this amount to get permission to 'export' what was in fact his own property. Karl said goodbye to his sister and they promised to see each other soon. Then Father took her to Düsseldorf to catch the boat train to England. The letters that came from her after she had arrived in the village of Elmhurst were cheerful and Father said contentedly, 'I knew they would be all right. I think people who use embossed letterheads are gentlefolk and they are bound to have decent standards. Now we must wait for your date of departure, Karl. Are you working on your new geometry book?'

Of course Karl said he was working, and his father said, 'Good,' but never probed any deeper. And so the prospect of going away gradually became more real. Karl would begin a sentence, 'Next year I will. . . .' and then say to himself, I don't really know where I will be next year, and that frightened him. He also realised that the dog could not come with him, and another thing that worried him was that his father was beginning to get rid of things in the house. 'There won't be room in Cecilia's house for all our things, some stuff will have to go. We have got the furniture and belongings of two households here.'

An advertisement went into the paper to say that furniture, books and porcelain were for sale. Father asked Grandfather Freudenberg if he would like to look after the selling and he was happy to do it. He was in his element selling and bargaining. It was like the good old days when he was running the store. A lot of people called. Some just walked round the house, asking, 'Is that for sale? How much?' Then Grandfather, who walked with them, named a price and they moved on.

Karl hated it all desperately. All the things for sale were part of his world and here, suddenly, strange people came and offered sums of money for them. One man called in the evening and he seemed terribly nervous. 'I don't like to be seen going into a Jewish house,' he said confidentially to Grandfather and after a few minutes he asked where the lavatory was and rushed in. When he came out again, he said he was a collector and some of the pieces were quite nice. He was particularly interested in the porcelain in the glass case.

'Ah, that's Meissen, what do you want for it?' Grandfather named a price and the man said, 'That's far too much, I have been to several Jewish houses and they are selling their things at much lower prices.'

Grandfather Freudenberg did not give way. 'But you see these are specially good pieces; you are one of the earliest purchasers. Perhaps you would like to think it over and come again tomorrow? Of course I can't guarantee that anything will be left by then.' The man made another trip to the lavatory. Grandfather said to Karl, 'He is a dealer and he is just taking advantage of the fact that we are having to sell everything.' The man returned and they agreed on a price.

More people came. Some asked if they had any copies of Heine. Heine, a Jew, was banned in Germany. His works had been burned on the bonfire at the beginning of Hitler's rule and his work was no longer available in bookshops, so now people wanted to buy his writings as collectors' pieces. They had two sets, one in the bookcase in the drawing room and another in the bookcase Karl had set up for himself in the living room after he had been given so many volumes for his barmitzvah. 'You can't take your books with you,' said his father 'so we might as well sell yours as well.' And in the end there were great gaps in the shelves, and the glass case in the drawing room was almost empty.

Karl found a box full of costumes which had belonged to his mother when she was a young girl. There were medieval dresses, rococo dresses and a clown's outfit. Karl decided to put on the medieval dress. It smelt of old perfume and was a bit stale and he could not do up the buttons and hooks at the back. He found some lipstick and he stuffed out the bosom with some rags and he went to Ella's room. He knocked on the door. There was some creaking of bed springs and some whispering and after quite some time the door opened. Ella had been entertaining a girl friend and there were two young men in the room as well. They all looked a bit dishevelled and embarrassed, but Karl minced in quite unconcerned, walked up and down and recited

> *I am Pauline Plumtree*
> *if you pay me handsomely*
> *I'll even show you where I pee.*

This was a great success and they roared with laughter and made a great fuss of Karl. Ella thought he looked just like a girl and wasn't he a lad. The men thought he was funny, too, and Karl thought he would complete the realism of the scene by climbing on to one of the men's knees, but was a bit discomfited when he felt his hard prick under him, so he excused himself and went back to his room. Later in the evening he heard his father come upstairs, knock on the door and say, 'This is a respectable house, will you kindly get out and get out immediately,' and they went. Ella seemed more disgruntled than usual the next morning and Karl heard his father say to his grandfather, 'The house is absolutely falling apart. This is no place for a boy to be growing up.' Grandfather agreed, and Karl was left wondering why there had been such a commotion.

One day late in April 1939 a letter came from England and it said that Karl was expected, that there was a place for him in Ramsgate and that he would be fetched from the station by Mr Selig who would put him on the train to Ramsgate. The date for departure was May 9, and suddenly everything became urgent. He had to get a customs form, a valuation form for what he was going to take with him, and a form to say that he left no debts and that all his taxes had been paid. Everything he did now seemed to be something that he was going to do for the last time. He went to the little stationery shop round the corner and bought a supply of drawing pencils and drawing paper. 'I won't be coming any more,' he announced, 'I am going to England.'

The lady whose shop it was looked round. There was no one else in the shop, 'I think it is a crying shame,' she said. 'I think it is terrible the way you people are being treated. I have known your family for years. Now your mother was a real lady and I was very sorry when she died. And they went into your house and smashed it all up, and they burned the Wallachs' house. I think it is terrible; they have no right to do all that. I hope you manage all right in England.' And she gave Karl a red and blue pencil as a going-away present.

Then there was Mr Charc. 'What a pity you are going! I would have made a champion weight-lifter out of you. You have got real potential. I think this place is going to the dogs. I have to get out of here just when I had built up a nice little practice. They say I can't stay in a Jew's house any more. I have got nothing against the Jews. You have all been my best customers and we have always got on well together.'

Karl nodded, he had a lump in his throat. He liked Mr Charc very much. He had never made fun of him and had always treated him as if he was a gifted athlete.

'Well goodbye, then, Karl, you'll be all right; you are the sort that always comes out on top. Good luck.' And they shook hands.

Karl also said his goodbyes at the small wooden hut where he used to eat his rolls and drink his cup of soup. The man said, 'Well, I am losing a good customer,' and they shook hands.

The dog worried Karl more than anything. 'What will you do?' he asked his father. 'I will take him for his walks in the evening but I am sure he will miss you.'

His father told him the travelling plans. 'I will take you to Cologne and there you will join the children's transport. A whole group of Jewish children is going at the same time. It will be nice for you to be travelling with so many young people. When you get to London you will be met by Mr Selig and he will see you across London and put you on the train to Ramsgate.' He showed Karl where Ramsgate was on the map and he gave him a thick envelope which had all the travel documents and tickets in it. Karl suddenly realised that he had still some money hidden away; he felt he could not give it back to his father because he would ask where it came from, and there were also several boxes of Abdullah cigarettes. He put the contraband into an empty cigar box and he went down to the boiler room and he threw the box on top of the red hot coke. It burned up quickly and reminded Karl of all the goldfish funerals he had conducted. Whenever a fish had died Karl had put it into a cigar box and cremated it, singing mournful religious dirges.

The next day the two smaller cases were standing in the hall and they were waiting for the taxi. 'The big case will come by Carter Paterson when you are settled in Ramsgate.' He hugged Grandfather Freudenberg, who gave him a stubbly kiss on the cheek and said, 'Goodbye, look after yourself, you will be all right. Write soon.' Karl promised he would.

Father had given him a small stack of international reply coupons which could be exchanged for stamps. Ella held out her hand. 'Good luck, boy, don't get into trouble and look after yourself.' The dog was whimpering in the bathroom. 'We'll have to leave him there or he will be too upset,' said his father. 'We had better go.'

They climbed into the taxi and Grandfather and Ella waved goodbye from the portico. He did not not know what to say to his father. He wanted to say, 'I am sorry I lied all the time and I am sorry I took all that money out of your pocket and I am sorry I did not do any geometry out of the English textbook. Will I ever see you again? And why are you staying behind?' Instead he listened to his father who so much wanted to give him advice that would keep him out of trouble. 'Never play around with firearms,' his father suddenly said, and he told him about a distant relative whose boy had played around with a gun and there was a bang and the boy was dead. Karl thought of the dismembered imitation pistol in the garden. 'And be good friends with your sister, you will have to look after each other from now onwards.'

They had a late breakfast on the station in Cologne and ate the same things as they had when they had the day out together; and then his father took him to the platform where there were many

Jewish families with their children. 'You must save as much money as you can,' his father said, in a hurry now. 'They have a saying in English, take care of the pence and the pounds will take care of themselves. You will need every penny as I can't give you any money to take with you.' Karl kissed his father on the cheek and he hugged him; he climbed into a compartment that was already full of children, and so he left.

Chapter 9

The train was full of children from all over Germany. A man came round and gave Karl a label and told him to fill it in and to tie it through his button hole. The other children in the compartment were very quiet, and they were all uncertain of what was going to happen. Karl filled the label in with his fountain pen: name, destination. It had Children's Transport printed on the top. The border came very soon and there did not seem to be many formalities. No one was searched. A policeman and a man in civilian clothes just went from compartment to compartment and counted. The train waited a bit and suddenly they saw that the policemen had different uniforms and the signs were in Dutch. One child said, 'We are out. We are in Holland.' Karl felt a bit blasé; he had been to Holland before. It was not all that far from Essen and they had made excursions over the frontier to have coffee and cake and to buy butter and eggs. A certain amount could be taken back to Germany and in the early days of the National Socialist government there had not been many restrictions.

The man who seemed to be in charge of the whole group came in and said, 'We are going to have a break in Amsterdam. You will have something to eat there, and then we are going on to the Hook and you will sleep on the boat tonight.' The children became excited. Lunch was an interesting prospect, and they began asking each other where they had come from and where they were going. In Amsterdam they were taken to a large hall, given something to eat, and then a lady came round and gave each child a bar of chocolate. 'From the Jewish community here with best wishes,' she said. Some children were already in the hall. They seemed to live there. The boys were wearing little skull caps and they looked pale and miserable. 'We are stuck here,' one of the boys told Karl, 'and we don't know where we are going. You are lucky, you are going to England and at least there is a bit of sea between you and those bastards.' Karl had, until then, not considered himself to be particularly lucky. He had just accepted that arrangements would be made for him and that everything would somehow work out all right. Here were children who were much worse off than he was.

When they had left the hall they were ferried on to another train and then to the boat. Karl felt stiff and uncomfortable, all his clothes were new and clean. He had the two suitcases which he could barely carry and now he had to find a cabin deep down in the ship. An older boy already had the bottom bunk and he scrambled to the top. He was not used to sharing with anybody else and he felt very bashful about undressing. He wriggled out of his clothes on the top bunk and as he put his new pyjamas on he tore them with a loud noise. The boy below shouted up, 'Stop farting will you,' and Karl felt mortified. In the early morning he went on deck just in time to see the ferry going into the harbour. He saw some fortifications with apertures for guns, and some pill boxes. A boy behind him said, 'Oh boy, they are prepared. They are armed to the teeth. The Germans will never try any funny stuff with the English, they are far too powerful.' Karl thought this was a happy thought and he decided that he had come to a safe place and that everything was going to be all right.

At Liverpool Street Station they were met and led to squares marked with letters. 'Wait here until you are collected,' they were told. They were also given paper bags with sandwiches and a piece of what Karl thought was very weird cake. 'With the compliments of the committee,' the lady who handed out the bags said. Suddenly Karl's name was called and he was face to face with Mr Selig, a harassed looking, pale young man with a very thin, fine-haired beard and a black hat with a wide rim.

149

'There you are, had a good trip? Well I am going to take you to Victoria Station now. I see you have got two suitcases, we had better take a taxi in that case. I will get the cost back on expenses.'

To Karl the air seemed acrid and everything looked rather yellow. He saw people hurrying about the City, and spotted the messengers with their top hats. His father had told him about the top hats. What seemed so extraordinary to Karl was that everyone was talking a language he could not understand. Mr Selig seemed to manage all right. When they got to Victoria he paid the driver and then turned to Karl. 'Have you got any money?' Karl said no, and he gave him a shilling. Karl turned it over in his hand and it seemed a strange new thing, a shilling – his very first piece of English money. 'And here, so that you can tell your parents you have arrived safely. . .' He handed Karl a small book of stamps. Karl had seen these stamps before because they had been part of his collection. He asked, 'What goes on a letter home?' and was shown the right stamp.

He was taken to the train that said Ramsgate on it and the bags were put inside. Mr Selig said, 'Good luck, goodbye,' and the train set off and Karl was really on his own. He felt as if he was in a dream. Here he was in another country, suddenly, only a day and a half away from home and everything was different. The people around him looked different, there was nothing that did not seem unfamiliar, even the notices in the train. He tried to decipher them but could only guess that one meant that it would be dangerous to stick his head out of the window. He kept on feeling in his pockets; yes his identity card was still there, so was the new shilling; and the suitcases were still there, one brown and big and the other smaller and black. He got out at Ramsgate and just stood there not knowing what to do next, and then a fair, thin boy came up to him and asked, 'Are you the new boy for the hostel, Karl Hartland?'

Karl could have hugged him, someone was expecting him and what was more he spoke German. It was a strange German to Karl and it appeared that Sigi had come from Vienna. He took the smaller case and Karl lugged the bigger one to a bus stop.

'What's the hostel like?' Karl wanted to know.

'All right, very nice,' said Sigi, 'the food is first class and we go to the beach quite often. The only trouble is jobs; they won't allow us to find jobs or to begin apprenticeships; only one of the lads has got an apprenticeship, so we just sit around and wait. We do a lot of housework, but in the afternoons we can get out.'

Karl said that he was expecting to start in a school.

'There's no school here, but we have English lessons every day; we are all learning English.'

The cases had to be carried up a hill and the hostel was in a Georgian terrace house overlooking the harbour.

The man who opened the door spoke German with a different accent. He introduced himself as Mr Kodak and then took Karl down to meet his wife. They explained that they were both refugees as well. Karl thought she was beautiful. She had very fair hair, an open round face with blue eyes, and she smiled at Karl. He was enchanted. 'You must be dead tired, come into our little room.' A small dog jumped up at Karl. 'That's Bobby.'

Karl said, 'He seems to know that I had a dog of my own, but he was huge, an Alsatian.'

The room he was going to occupy was shared with two other boys. There were just beds, and in front of each bed stood a large locker which Mr Kodak called 'your troenk'. Downstairs was a lounge for the boys and a quiet room 'where you can study or write your letters'. Mr Kodak explained that he was a Hungarian, had lived in Berlin for some years after fleeing from the revolution in Hungary, and had been a fencing champion. His wife was not Jewish at all. She came from East Germany. The Germans did not like 'mixed marriages' and they told her to leave him, but they stayed together.

There were seventeen boys in the hostel and at the evening meal Karl was introduced. 'This is Karl; he is from Essen, and I think he is the youngest now.' He got interested looks from some of the boys but then they got on with the meal. Mr Kodak explained one rule. 'We don't talk at meals, it gets too noisy, and I want to be able to talk to each of you and to my wife.'

There was some pudding left over and Mr Kodak got out a little black book. 'We must explain to Karl how we do things here. Everything has got to be fair . . .' he used the English word . . . 'We keep a list and when a boy has a second helping we put a tick against his name.' Karl thought that this seemed a fair arrangement. He had never been with so many young people except at school, but here they were all refugees and it seemed that a number came from Austria as well as Germany.

In his bedroom he wrote home on his knee: 'I have arrived safely. It is very nice here. There is a dog called Bobby and we had liver and fried potatoes for supper and for pudding we had something that was pink and tasted of raspberries. I will write again soon.'

His two room mates came in; one was Sigi and the other Peter, both from Austria. Karl thought their way of talking was weird, but they thought the same about his German. 'You talk like a proper Imperial German Prussian,' they said. Karl pointed out that Essen was in fact in Westphalia. 'Ah,' Sigi said, 'Westphalian ham.'

They talked about the hostel and seemed very contented with it. 'If only there were some girls,' Peter sighed, 'it gets lonely without girls and we are not allowed to go out in the evening; they are strict about that. They say we must not do anything to draw attention to ourselves or to annoy the neighbours.' Peter was at least sixteen and was handsome. He had curly hair and a tanned complexion.

Karl was transferring his things into the box. His suitcases were to go into the store, he had been told, and Mr Kodak said, 'Don't put all your clothes out; have some old stuff for the house and one suit for good, but save your things, it will be difficult to replace them.'

Two boys were working, one at a garage and another with a firm of electricians. They were much respected and they came back in the evening with tales of what England was like, what their workmates said to them and what they were doing. Peter and Sigi were a bit envious of them. They would have liked to have learnt a trade but like the majority in the hostel there was nothing for them. Sigi took Karl to post his first letter home. The postbox, he noticed, was red and round and not yellow and square. Karl felt uncertain about going out; he did not know enough English to ask his way back, and so he waited until another boy took him along.

Gradually he got to know the different boys. They came up to him, asked him where he was from, what he was going to do and did he like it here. There were two brothers, Martin and Ernst Wald; they came from Duisburg which was not far from Essen. They said, 'Oh yes, we have heard your name; the bankers, aren't you?' Karl always suspected that when people said that to him they meant the other Hartlands and not his father's rather smaller bank, but he just accepted the fact that he was someone whose family was known. Martin said he wanted to become a rabbi. He had already finished at his gymnasium and had taken his final leaving examination. He had a broad grin and a friendly face and he asked Karl whether he had had his barmitzvah and was he orthodox. This sort of questioning made Karl uneasy. He did not want to go on with religion and religious classes and he felt he was going to be drawn into more religious activity. Martin said after that a few of the boys went to a synagogue and would he like to come. Karl did not want to, but he wanted to make friends and so he said that he would come along the next Friday.

The younger brother was one of the two boys doing an apprenticeship and he seemed more humorous and easy-going than his brother. He said to Karl, 'Keep away from Harry, he is a wanker.'

'A what?'

'A wanker, polishes the old maypole every night.' Ernst made the appropriate rhythmic gesture with his hand. 'Know what I mean?'

It was clear to Karl that this had something to do with the great mystery and was connected with sex, but he could not bear to admit ignorance so he tried to seem knowing and just said, 'Oh.'

At supper he looked at Harry discreetly; he had dark hair

and rather pink skin and the beginnings of a moustache on his upper lip. He seemed all right, but Karl decided to be careful. Neither of the Walds had much time for Viennese boys. 'Common most of them, just from the slums.' And they made it clear that they must present a common front against these people with a strange accent and words that were quite new to Karl.

In the evening Peter suddenly leant out of the window. 'There she is again. Oh boy, it's the one with the green coat.' There was a street lantern on the promenade in front of the house and there was a bench under it on which two girls were lounging. The green one had reddish hair, and when Peter whistled she looked up and laughed. He leant out of the window until he nearly fell out, 'Oh God! If I could only get to her; that sod, Kodak, would kick me out, though. He said that if any boy goes out without permission he will have him kicked out, and where the hell can we go if we can't stay here?'

Karl leant over Peter to have a good look at the girl. He did not think she was all that marvellous but he did not want to be thought anything less than a man of the world. That night, when he was already half asleep, he felt that his prick was large and he began to pull at it and then he could not stop any more; suddenly there was an almighty explosion and then he lay still. He could feel that it was wet and sticky all over his stomach and was frightened. 'Oh God! I have torn something, I am covered in blood,' he thought, and he wondered how he was going to get medical aid for such an intimate wound. How could he go up to Mrs Kodak and say. . . . So he decided to go to the lavatory and have a look. He was sure it was blood, like the time when he had cut his forehead and Grandmother Freudenberg nearly had hysterics. To his relief he found no blood and realised that all this had something to do with the mysterious 'wanking' he had been warned about. He decided to try again the next night to see if it worked. He was a bit worried because he did not want to get known for this activity, but he also decided that it was too good to miss. Sigi certainly talked about it much more happily than Martin, and all the boys made jokes about it. Karl felt that now he had joined the club.

Letters came from home. His father wrote every day, sometimes not letters but pre-paid letter cards; the two cards could be separated leaving a clean one on which the postage had been paid in advance. His father told him of the move to Aunt Cecilia's flat:

'At her age she has decided to dye her hair red, she will become a beauty in her old age. We had cabbage and potatoes mixed together the way you like them with boiled sausages. I took Pisser for a walk, but he puts he head sideways, and looks at me quizzically as if to say, "Where is my master?" Are you working hard? Are you preparing for school? How are the English lessons?'

The English lessons were late in the afternoon and were taken by a teacher from the local grammar school. He was an elderly man and he made little jokes the boys found hard to understand. No doubt he went away convinced that Germans had no sense of humour. They used a very old English textbook and they did exercises like *A lot of bees are a ......, A lot of sheep are a ......* and what does *He is in a brown study* mean and *His face is as black as......*

Karl was a long way behind the other boys who had either done more English at their schools or had been at the hostel longer. Gradually some of the words made more sense and he read copies of *Picture Post* which were available in the boys' common room. He saw that there were articles that were very critical of Nazi Germany and this excited him enormously. He had only heard very subdued criticism of the regime at home. He knew that all their Jewish friends and relatives were unhappy and hated the regime that was so hostile to them, but nothing was ever explicit. No one ever explained to him exactly what was wrong. He knew about Dachau because Ella's boy friend had been there, and it was sometimes said that a certain person had 'disappeared'. But here were specific accounts and attacks on the Fascists. Everything was seen from a different point of view; the Spanish Civil War, which in

Germany was reported like a war of liberation with Franco as the liberator, was here seen as an attack on a legitimate government. The boys saw cartoons by Low and they were enormously amused and excited by them. It had certainly never occurred to Karl that those who had governed him could be either absurd or lunatic.

The Kodaks put up lists for housework and each week Karl was assigned to different duties. In the first week it was the staircase. He had to go from top to bottom with a little dustpan and brush; after that he had to dust furniture and then all the brass had to be polished. Mrs Kodak was strict. She wiped her hand over ledges and made a boy do his job all over again if he had left any dirt.

The week after that he was in the kitchen. He liked that because he could talk to Mrs Kodak, and while he was shaving thick wedges of peel off the potatoes he would listen to her talk about Germany and Hungary. All the boys liked to talk about their homes, except for Karl who was afraid they would tease him. There had already been one or two remarks about his rich father and about being a spoilt mother's boy. This was because there was a letter for him every day. 'I don't know how your parents can afford the postage,' said Sigi rather enviously.

The other problem was the Walds, who were regarded as prigs, Martin with his aspirations to rabbinical office and Ernst because of his apprenticeship. Karl went to the synagogue with them. It was a marble-lined place and there were two problems for Karl – although he did not understand what went on in Hebrew, still he was used to it from home and that helped, but the English part escaped him completely.

He began to be more confident and in the afternoon he was now prepared to go out on his own. He ventured into Woolworths which was full of a strange smell and piles upon piles of sweets. Karl's father had put a couple of bags of mints in his suitcase but they were soon gone.

The boys were given a shilling pocket money a week. They could either take the money or have it credited in a little booklet, and Mr Kodak would pay out any sums they asked for.

Peter, who was more independent, took his shilling and blued it on chocolate. Karl desperately wanted to save some money and each week another shilling would be added to his pile; he was mindful of his father's warnings. In fact in his postcards from home his father would ask repeatedly; 'How are your savings? Soon you will have a pound. When you have, take it away from Mr Kodak (not that I don't trust him) and put it into a post office savings account and then you will get two-and-a-half per cent interest and your money will be quite safe.'

Unexpectedly Karl became wealthy by hostel standards. He received a registered letter from London and there were two new pound notes in it. These had been sent to him by order of his father's best friend who lived in Paris. Margot had told Karl about him. 'A real rake,' she said with awe, 'lives with a mistress and he has always lived in high style.' Father had asked if he would help with Karl's education, but the two pounds were the only response. Karl was delighted. He opened his post office savings account and spent sixpence on a bar of Cadbury's chocolate. His father told him what to write in his thank you letter. 'Say: you and I have the same name and an appendix scar in the same spot. I am sorry we have never met but many thanks for the cash.'

Most of his father's postcards still exhorted him to save and Karl felt like answering back, 'It's all right for you to preach but you don't walk around the sweet counters and you don't want to go to the cinema.' He went with Sigi and Peter to see a film called *Beau Geste* and this was a tremendous experience. No cinema Karl had ever been to before had an organist who came up from below, and the film was exciting, specially when the thief was fixed to the table top with a bayonet and the evil sergeant was laid at the foot of Beau Geste's brother's funeral pyre. They came out of the cinema elated.

The English lessons went on and one day the teacher shocked Martin Wald: the other boy who was working in a garage asked if the word 'bugger' could be explained and the teacher seemed very happy to furnish an explanation. He said it was something to do with the Bulgars who the English thought had some frightful habits. 'Men made love to each other there,' he added looking very salacious. Martin was full of indignation. 'A teacher has no right to talk about indecent things like that, we must report the matter to Mr Kodak, the man is not fit to teach young men.' Karl did not see what all the fuss was about, but Martin asked if he would come along and complain, and he felt it very difficult to oppose Martin who was so much older and who was going to be a rabbi. Also his father had contacted the Wald parents. They had met and were pleased that the boys were such good friends. Karl hated to complain but he went along and stood by the door and Martin made his speech. Mr Kodak did not seem terribly impressed but said he would think about what Martin had told him and see what could be done. He added that the teacher was doing the lessons as a favour almost, and for very little money indeed.

Later Karl was walking along the sea front with Martin, when he suddenly put his arm round him and said, 'Do you believe in God, Karl?' Karl was again embarrassed and said he was thinking about the problem and could not say immediately.

'But you must believe or life has no meaning and there is no sense in morality. You are very young and you must be protected against immorality.'

He was holding Karl very tightly, and Karl hated it but remembered that the Walds had had a food parcel that morning. They had aunts somewhere in England who sent them all sorts of good things, including liver sausage, and Martin had promised Karl some. It was a difficult situation and Karl felt deeply uncomfortable.

'I tell you what,' said Martin, 'we will walk together again tomorrow and you can tell me then whether you really believe or not,' and he went on about the suffering of the Jewish people. Karl agreed about the suffering but he also remembered what Aunt Flora's husband had said when his little boy had died, and he wanted to say, 'If God is so good why all the suffering?'

The next day Martin asked him to come for a walk, and asked Karl what he had decided.

'Yes, I believe in God,' said Karl, and thought, 'I'm sure I don't, and if there is a God he should strike me with lightning now, because I have lied and denied his existence.' Lightning did not strike and Martin grasped Karl and Karl just felt embarrassed and hoped this sort of thing would not happen again.

After all the lonely and friendless years at home he was almost intoxicated with having friends around him, boys who teased him and pushed him around but did not very often taunt him. The great game in the hostel was snatching at other boys' genitals, and pretending to knock them in the balls, and then they would bend forward in mock agony or try to hit back. So whenever they met in the corridor they would make quick grabs at each other, and it was thought particularly hilarious to snatch at someone carrying a tray or otherwise encumbered. When Mrs Kodak was about they would do it behind her back and the stifled giggles became intense. She was particularly nice to Karl and this made another boy, Richard, jealous, but Karl did not really take any notice of his jealousy. She would ask Karl to do special things for her in the kitchen, and Richard would be on the other side of the table glowering and sulking. He had thin, very curly hair and was about seventeen. 'Come on, let's wrestle,' he said to Karl when they were fooling around on the beach one day. And Karl suddenly realised that this was not just for fun. Richard was throwing him down hard and suddenly he had Karl's face in the sand and he kept on pushing. It needed all Karl's strength to get his head up and he was frightened. 'Come on, I thought this was only for fun,' he pleaded, but Richard went on at him hard and Karl tried to wrestle with more strength and purpose. Suddenly Richard got Karl's arm and twisted it behind his back and it really hurt, Karl let out a howl and some of the other boys stopped the fight. 'Come on, Richard, that's not fair, you are much older, don't be such a sod.'

The boys used the word 'fair' a lot, even when they were talking in German which they did most of the time; but they said 'fair' in English. They had a strong impression that England was a place where justice and fair play meant something, and they were continually surprised that they were included in the provisions made by the government. They were really touched, when they, too, received their gas masks in little cardboard boxes. Peter said, 'They are decent. At home they would have said Jews can't have any or they would have made us pay for them.'

Karl viewed England as a good and benevolent place; he and the other boys were constantly telling each other how the English gave Jews equal rights, and they were impressed that Hore-Belisha, at that time minister in charge of the War Office, was a Jew. Had not the traffic beacons been named after him? Then there was Disraeli – Karl's father had already told him about this prime minister and how he obtained money for the Suez Canal from the Rothschilds.

'How much money do you need, Mr Disraeli?' asked old Rothschild.

'Five or six million pounds.'

'What is your security?'

'The British Empire.'

Old Rothschild spat a grape pip into his hand and said, 'Done.'

The boys discovered that the editor of *Picture Post* was a refugee and it seemed to them that England was the land of opportunity and fair play.

Karl met his first 'Englishman'. He was a boy scout called Albert, who invited the boys to join the nearby scout troop. He was very fair, almost red haired, and Karl decided that all 'typical' Englishmen had light complexions and fair hair. The boys went along to the scout hall and played around with the gym equipment. Karl ran up against the leather covered horse as ineffectively as he had done at home, but everyone here thought it was a good joke and no one teased him. They played tag, chased each other, ragged and wrestled, and Karl was desperately anxious to understand what the English boys were saying to him. They all smiled, gesticulated, shrugged and cheered when Karl said, 'Thank you very much.' Albert came to the hostel and they sat him in the front room and treated him like a precious and important yet fragile museum piece. Here was a real Englishman and he had come to their hostel. Albert was clearly uncomfortable and did not know what to do, but there was so much good will on both sides they carried on as best they could. 'That's a really nice chap,' said Sigi with conviction, 'you can rely on people like that.'

Karl got into trouble. He was so intoxicated with having other boys around that he became more and more boisterous. He was the most active in the 'ball snatching' games, he jostled and fought more than most, and now he irritated Mr Kodak with what he called 'idiocies'. The boys had almost developed a comic language of their own, it was based on Viennese pronunciation which they imitated in a way they thought was very comical. Instead of 'potatoes' they would say 'bhuddodies', and then there would be shrieks of laughter. Mr Kodak could not stand it. 'Stop these idiocies,' he would suddenly snap at dinner. His eyes were dark and seemed to glitter with anger, his grey-black hair, which had receded quite a way from his forehead, stood on end. 'I demand that this foolishness stops. Karl come and see me afterwards, you seem to be one of the ring-leaders.'

Karl went into the little sitting room feeling very heavy legged and fearful of what would happen. Would he be expelled? Sometimes Mr Kodak would hint darkly that boys could be removed from the hostel if he chose to suggest it to the management committee. The committee, it appeared were a group of London doctors who had made contributions to start the hostel and who supported it.

'Karl, you must be more serious,' said Mr Kodak. He didn't seem to be all that angry. 'You are very young and the older boys are teaching you silly ways, you must take life more seriously.'

Karl felt tears rising in his eyes and he promised hotly that from now onwards he would be serious. He noticed a pile of chocolate bars next to Mr Kodak's chair. Surely, he thought, this fencing champion does not eat chocolate like a little boy? Will he offer me some? But Karl was dismissed. 'Think of your father and your family: they want you to learn something and be somebody.' This was too much in front of Mrs Kodak, who was in the kitchen with her back turned to him. The humiliation was terrible. He hated to be told off with her in the kitchen and he just crept out of the room and locked himself in the lavatory and cried and cried. It was the first time he had really cried and it all came out; his sorrow at leaving home, his loneliness and his feelings of guilt at not pleasing those in authority, and his rage at those who made him do things he did not want to do. He felt empty and changed when he came out of the lavatory. Sigi asked, 'What's up, you look different, have you been crying?' 'Of course not,' snapped Karl, 'what have I got to blub about?'

Sigi was not to be deterred. 'What did he say to you? Why has he made you so unhappy?' But Karl just said that Mr Kodak had told him not to fool around so much.

'Oh him,' scoffed Sigi. 'He wants us to be quiet and nice all the time so that he can live here like a gentleman of leisure. We disturb him and he can't go on pretending he is the lord of the manor, and that blonde tart of his.'

Karl felt outraged. 'He runs this place very well and the food is good, even you must admit that. That's the trouble with you Viennese, always moaning and groaning, and you don't do your share of the work either.' This was more what Karl had heard from the Walds than his own opinion, but he thought Sigi was stirring things up and that it wasn't fair.

'That's right, be a good little boy, mummy's darling, just be nice and you will get lots of sweeties.'

They were on the verge of fighting each other but the steam went out of their anger. 'Come on, let's go for a walk,' said Sigi.

They had a look at the shelters that were dug underneath Ramsgate. The town stood on chalk, and deep air raid shelters were being dug out and lorries took the chalk away and dumped it. 'I hope we will be safe in those,' said Sigi.

The war seemed inevitable and everyone talked about it. There were special anti-gas respirators for babies and each boy had the yellowish cardboard box with a respirator in it standing by his bedside. Karl's father wrote of dark clouds and thunderstorms gathering and that there might be a storm soon. This was the double language they had learnt to speak and understand in Germany. No one dared to say anything directly. Karl was reminded of Margot's fear when he told her that his father had 'gone away', which she had immediately understood to mean that he had been arrested, when in fact he had just gone into hiding. Karl found it more and more difficult to write home, it was as if he was rehearsing the total break that was bound to come. He hated the cards that came every day, questioning him closely on what he was doing: was he working hard? Was he reading the geometry book? (It lay unopened in Karl's trunk). Was he saving his money and not spending it on inessentials? The heels on Karl's shoes needed repairing and Ernst showed him how he could mend them himself. Karl bought a pice of hard rubber the same size as the heel of his shoe, which had a screw hole in the middle. When the heel had been screwed on Ernst explained, 'You turn the piece round, so it's much more economical than the ordinary heel.' Soles could also be bought and were glued on to the shoe and then the sole was further secured with a few nails. Karl, who had never known such economies, was intrigued.

Margot announced that she would visit Karl in Ramsgate and he was surprised to find how pleased and excited he was at the prospect of seeing her. He found a room for her in a nearby hotel and she came late in the afternoon.

'Oh, baby rabbit, how you have grown, and you are so thin,' she shouted when she saw Karl in the hall. Karl saw the evil grin on Sigi's face and knew that he would be 'baby rabbit' to his 'friends' for a long time to come. He had grown and, by the standards of his family he was positively a giant at five foot seven. He was certainly a head taller than his sister now and he was thinner. Not being able to rifle the fridge or to buy sweets at all times had reduced him, although the food at the hostel was good and plentiful.

Margot was wearing her smart grey costume. 'Do you know,' she said, 'it was funny; when I got out of the train at Victoria I was met by Mrs Barratt and she was wearing the same outfit! I don't think she has liked me ever since that moment.'

It seemed that Margot was not nearly as happy in her place as a maid servant as her letter home had suggested. 'I just didn't want to worry Father,' she said, 'it must be bad enough for him to have to go on living in Essen, so I just tell him everything is lovely.'

She shared an attic with a girl she didn't like at all, the work was boring, she had broken some of the best Wedgwood china and they only paid her fifteen shillings a week. When the family went on holiday they gave her even less, ten shillings because after all there was no work to do. Then there was a nanny who thought she was better than the maids, and who reported them for anything they did wrong. The Barratts had two nice children and she would have liked to talk to them but whenever they came near nanny would appear as if from nowhere and shoo the children away. Mrs Barratt drank, and every evening Margot had to go to her bedroom with a huge tray of drinks, then in the morning she would find the bottles half-empty and Mrs Barratt bad-tempered and bossy.

Karl told her all about the hostel and introduced Margot to the Kodaks, and he hoped Mr Kodak would not tell her about his misdeeds. On the contrary, Mr Kodak brought out unsuspected reserves of charm and invited them both to sit down. They had coffee and he talked about his fencing and the fencing school he had run in Berlin and how he expected to open one in England before long. When they left the Kodaks and Karl was walking Margot to the hotel she said, 'I am glad I am not sleeping in the same house as that ram. I bet he would be knocking at my door; and doesn't he seem to think he is the greatest ever. As they say, a refugee dachshund can boast "in Berlin I was a St Bernard".' Karl was amused and shocked, but his sister was now talking to him as if he was adult and it amazed him that she could be so critical of anyone so quickly.

In the hostel Sigi's hostility to the Kodaks became a propaganda campaign. 'Have you ever looked in the box room?' The box room was where the boys kept their spare clothes and suitcases. It was kept locked, but they could go in if Mr Kodak went in with them. 'Well,' said Sigi, 'I looked round the door the other day – it had been left open. And what do you know, there are stacks and stacks of clothes in there. They have been sent to us by charity people; all sorts of things, pullovers and scarves and spare jackets, and they have never given them to us, have they?'

'But we don't need clothes,' said Karl.

'You may not because your parents are rich and you have suitcases full of stuff, but my parents did not buy me much. They couldn't and a pullover would be useful, especially when winter comes.'

'Perhaps they will give them out when winter comes.'

'Yeah! We'll be lucky. They are keeping it all for themselves. they will flog all that stuff, you'll see.'

A few days later Karl was working on the stairs and he saw the door of the store room open. He heard the Kodaks talking downstairs, so he slid into the room. Sigi was right; there were all sorts of clothes on the shelves. 'I'll take a pullover for Sigi,' Karl thought to himself, and took a pullover without sleeves. Once he was outside the room he was panic-stricken. Why had he done it? He certainly did not need a pullover himself, and why should he risk getting into trouble for Sigi's sake? What had got into him? By the time he had decided to take it back the room was locked again, so Karl stuffed the stolen pullover at the bottom of his locker.

A few days later at dinner Mr Kodak had a very dark and angry face, 'I must tell you something, and it isn't pleasant. There is a thief among us and I want to know who it is. There were some clothes in the store room which I was saving for you for the winter.' Karl looked at Sigi whose lip curled slightly. 'I checked them the other day and a pullover is missing. Who took it?'

Karl felt he could not possibly admit his theft. He had not passed the pullover on to Sigi and had not mentioned to him that he had been in the room.

'Come on, now, who took it?'

Uncomfortable silence.

'I'll tell you what I will do, I will ask the two senior boys to go upstairs and look into every locker and I warn you, when I find out who did it I will take that boy down to the police station.'

Karl felt weak as he watched Martin and another boy go upstairs for their search. He thought to himself, 'If they find it I will just deny that I took it. I will say someone else put it there. I will just faint!' He could not move and just wanted to be somewhere else.

After some time Martin and the other reappeared and said they had found nothing. Mr Kodak said, 'Well it's not nice to think that there is a thief among you; why didn't whoever took it come to me and say, I need some clothes. I would have given him what he wanted.'

Sigi spoke up. 'But you have never told us that we could have anything from that store.'

'I forbid you to criticise the way I am running this hostel. If there are people here who don't like the way I am running the place, please leave. You are free to go any time you like, and then you will see what the world is really like. Who do you think you are, anyhow, always complaining, always finding something to criticise.'

'I only meant,' Sigi came back weakly, 'that we didn't know about the things. I like it here and I think you are running the place splendidly.'

Karl felt wretched because he knew all this would not have happened if he had kept his thieving fingers to himself. Next time he was alone in his room he took the pullover out and threw it down the stairwell; now anyone might have taken it.

Sigi showed his anger when he was in the room alone with Karl. 'He doesn't like me because I come from a poor part of Vienna. I bet they searched my locker more thoroughly than yours, and I bet he thought it was me. Well next time that damned place is open I will get in and take handfuls of stuff and old Kodak can kiss my arse.'

The boys went to the beach as often as they could. Karl

looked longingly at the people around him. They seemed so far away and with their own language which he could only partly understand, they and their whole lives were a mystery to him. What is it like when they get home, he wondered. Would it be like his home or different? He wanted them to appreciate him, to know that they had won an important ally in their fight against Nazism, but they did not seem worried whatever the newspapers said. Ernst explained that it was the famous British phlegmatic temperament. 'They just never get really excited. They keep calm and they don't shout at you. I find that at my work; they talk very quietly and you never really know what they think.'

Karl hoped that a child would nearly drown, so that he could dive into the sea and rescue it, give it artificial respiration and bring it back to life among a crowd of admirers; perhaps there would even be a medal from the king. He looked around the beach intently every day but nothing happened. There were just people in deck chairs and children eating ice cream. He would have liked a toffee apple but did not dare to spend any more of his money.

Poland was invaded, the ultimatum given and war declared. Karl looked over the Channel. It was a grey day and he knew that everything was going to change and he was anxious about what would happen to him. The sirens went a few minutes after Chamberlain had made his announcement and they all rushed to their rooms for their gas masks and stood in the shelter that was now finished. It was just bare chalk, it smelt wet and the light was yellow from small bulbs. The entrance had blankets over it; to keep the gas out, Sigi said. They just stood there and waited for the bombs to fall about them. No one said very much to anyone else and then the all clear went after half an hour and they went back to the hostel. The next day two plain-clothes policemen called and said that there had been a report that someone was sketching the harbour from one of the windows. Karl was fetched down and they asked to see his drawing book. He had been sitting in his room, and he had tried to draw the harbour and the ships. The policemen looked at all his sheets of drawing paper, searched his locker and then left again. 'You see,' said Mr Kodak to all the boys, 'they are watching us all the time, they do it quietly and without fuss, but they watch us all the time.'

Chapter 10

After the first dramatic air raid warning the war went on very quietly indeed. Karl read about it in *Picture Post*, saw the diagrams of the Maginot line and thought that it would stop any trouble if the Germans tried to break through. He drew complicated lines of fortifications on the side of his exercise book, and war at the moment did not seem as dreadful as all that. The main problem was the blackout. Every evening each window had to be thickly covered with blankets and curtains so that no light could get out. 'We must be doubly careful,' said Mr Kodak. 'They will think we are going to send signals up to bombers if we let light through.'

Every boy had certain windows to look after, and Karl's was the hall and the upstairs lavatory. There the window had to have a blanket; the blanket was held in its place with drawing pins, and there was a shortage of drawing pins in the hostel. Karl hid his right above the cistern and whenever he saw any other drawing pins he would hoard them. He spent quite a lot of time in that lavatory and was worried that he would become known as 'the wanker' in the hostel. Most of the boys always talked as if it was someone else who did it, and Karl was furious with Sigi when he said, 'You grow hair in the palms of your hand if you wank.' Karl, like a fool, had looked at the palm of his hand, and Sigi had shrieked with laughter and said, 'Caught you!'

The headmaster of the school Karl was supposed to go to had visited him one day. Karl didn't like him, particularly because when they walked along the deserted sea front he was eating plums out of a paper bag and did not offer him a single one.

Since he was quite small Karl had had strong feelings about sharing. Once he had refused to share his chocolate Easter eggs, and Malli had taken the box out of his hand and had offered each person in the room an egg. In the end there was just one left for him. If he had to share his sweets, so should others. He was outraged by the meanness of this man, and not entirely surprised that he never heard from him again.

The green geometry book still haunted Karl. It was in his locker and every time he saw it he felt guilty. Sometimes he turned the pages over. Once he asked Martin, who had already taken his final secondary education certificate, to help him. Martin tried, but his patience ran out very quickly when he realised that Karl lacked all understanding of mathematical principles in German, let alone in English.

No further letters came from home, just occasionally red cross letters with twenty-five words of type, like a telegram; just phrases like, 'I am well', 'I am going for walks'. 'Your aunt is well'.

Karl had mixed feelings about the letters; on the one hand he felt a sense of relief that the daily barrage of postcards had stopped. He had begun to dread the exhortations to save and to work, and on the other hand he missed hearing from his father and reading what his dog had been doing and what they had all eaten for their lunch. He wrote back on the same form his father's letter had been written on and said equally commonplace things, he hoped to please his father by adding that he was working hard. In fact his main work was keeping the house clean; each week's different routine meant that Karl learnt to scrub floors and wash the handkerchiefs and underpants of the other boys when he was on washing duty. He walked around the town in the afternoon, looking for Peter's green girl. But since the blackout the lantern outside had gone out and they could not lean out of the window any more.

One evening after supper Mr Kodak said, 'I have an important announcement to make. The hostel has to shut down. It was supported by a group of Jewish doctors in London, many of whom have been called up into the army. There is no money left and we have to close. You will be transferred to a farm camp near Oxford and you will have an opportunity to train for farm work there.'

'What will you do?' asked Martin.

'Oh, I have been preparing to leave for some time,' said Mr Kodak jauntily. 'I am planning to open a fencing academy in London, there will be good opportunities there.'

He sounded unconvincing and Karl realised, perhaps for the first time, the grown-ups felt insecure too – that they too could not always deal with events adequately. The boys met in small groups all over the hostel and there was much speculation and secret depression. The hostel had been a good place, it was beautifully situated, the boys had been well fed and comfortable and even if most of them had not received any training for a trade, they realised this was not the fault of the people running the place. There was also much grumbling. 'They are just getting rid of us to save a few pounds,' said Sigi. 'They took us on and now they are bored with us. I don't want to be a shitty farm labourer.'

Martin counselled moderation and reason. 'They can't keep us here for ever and it will be an interesting experience,' he said, without much conviction. He admitted to Karl that he now felt he would never have his chance of getting into a seminary where he could study to be a rabbi. Karl just felt lost. He had come to like the place, he had helped to keep it clean. There were the drawing pin pricks in the lavatory, almost a score board for his other activity there, where he could see how many times he had put up the blackout curtains. In the bedroom there was a big patch in the wall. He had been ragging with Peter one evening and during the fight had put his foot through the thin plaster and lattice wall. 'You can jolly well mend that out of your own money,' Mr Kodak had said, and so Karl had bought a packet of pink plaster – it was a surprising discovery to find that plaster in England was pink, at home it had been white – and had unskilfully covered the hole. Then he had found a roll of old wall-paper that matched and pasted it over. The patch was a reminder of the fight and made the room more his own.

Suddenly it was time to leave; the closing down of the hostel came much more quickly than Karl had expected. One morning they were told to pack their trunks and that a coach would take them to Wallingford after lunch. He went into the store room to get the brown trunk and the black case and Karl did not dare to look up to see if the pullovers were on the shelf. He just dragged the cases out and put his things in. He had mainly worn old things for doing the housework and had stopped wearing the plus-fours Margot had ordered for him. When they went out boys in the street had shouted 'Jerries' after them, and they decided it was the baggy trousers that gave them away, that and the hats. Karl had one with a small rim and an Edelweiss in the hat-band which was a thick green cord. He threw the hat into the dustbin and felt that he had gone a good step forward in his ac-climatisation as an Englishman. 'What sort of clothes will we wear for farm work?' he had asked, but no one had a clear idea and they did not really know what the next place was going to be. 'At best,' Sigi thought, 'it will be like this – a sort of hostel, and we go out and learn about farming. By the way, he didn't give out the pullovers, did he?'

The farewell from the Kodaks was brief, they said they were staying behind a day or two, just to clean the place up and no doubt they would all meet again and all the best and good luck and the coach set off.

They were taken to a group of wooden huts set apart from large blocks of barrack-like brick buildings.

'Here you are, lads,' said the driver, 'take your stuff off the coach, I have got to get back.'

They lugged the cases off, left them in a pile and were approached by a middle-aged man who was a refugee He told them he was in charge of the camp. 'A camp,' Karl wondered. 'What is a camp?' The explanation made everything clear: 'This is an approved school. It is really for English boys who are orphans, or who have been in some sort of trouble. They are trained for farm work here. A lot of them go to Australia after the training and if you become proficient farmers you may get the chance to go, too. It's a good opportunity, you can get good jobs there. First take your trunks to the store room and just take out a few things; clothes will be provided, good clothes, too, just right for farm work.'

The boys were too stunned to say very much, and they followed him to the store. Karl just took a few of his old clothes and put them into his little black case. It was difficult to choose, and in the end he could hardly close the case.

'Come on, I'll show you your beds.'

They were taken into a huge barrack room. It smelt of pine and creosote and sweaty feet. There were bunks, and Karl (it seemed to be his fate in life) was allotted the top bunk. It was terribly high. Sigi was on the top bunk next to him. All the boys from the hostel were in the same corner.

'You will meet the other lads at teatime when they come back from the fields, or wherever they have been working. We have a system of incentives here. If you keep tidy you get your full pocket money. You start off as unskilled at 3d per week, and then you go up as you become better at your work. The best boys can get as much as 1s 6d per week, but that takes time. The best job is in the cowsheds. If you do anything wrong you get fined; bed untidy a halfpenny, dirty necks a halfpenny, boots not clean for inspection a halfpenny. You have a chart in your hut which the hut leader keeps to make sure you do all the jobs. Now I will take you for your tea before the others get back.'

They tripped after the man down the hill to a one storey brick building. 'You won't see much of the English lads, keep out of their way and don't get into any fights. We play them at football and we won last week.'

There were bare trestle tables in the dining hall; they were given huge porcelain mugs of sweet tea and thick slices of white bread. Margarine here did not taste as desirable as Karl had thought it to be at home, and there was a dab of red jam. The plates were made of enamel and everything smelt of disinfectant; it was a bare place. They ate their tea and then were taken to the clothes store. Karl was given a short brown jacket made of corduroy, knee breeches which laced up below the knee, thick woollen stockings, heavy black boots and grey shirts which had no collar. There were also huge grey nightshirts.

'They are stiff, so you can't get your naughty little hands underneath,' Sigi said. 'How do you like the latest fashions?'

'Laundry is once a week. You put your things in a bundle and put a label with your name on the bundle, one shirt, one pair of pants, handkerchiefs and every fortnight your nightshirt. If you want to wear your own things you will have to wash them yourselves, but don't do it. You will be too tired to do much washing. If you work all right and behave yourselves you can get a pass to go into the town on Saturday afternoons. Not much on there but you can spend your pocket money if you want. You can't leave the camp without permission.'

Karl took his pile of new clothes back to the hut. He had three rough blankets and the mattress was filled with straw; he could feel the straw as he spread the blankets out and put his silk scarf over the pillow. It was all clean, but he did not like touching any of the things he had been given, they felt stiff and scratchy.

Sigi saw his hesitation, 'Ho, ho! The princess who couldn't sleep because there was a pea under the mattress; poor little Karl, all a bit rough for you?'

Karl was near tears. This was too true and he did not know what to do next. He clambered up to his high bed. 'Hope you don't wet the bed in your sleep,' came a cheerful cry from underneath.

Karl was just considering what would happen if he woke up, forgot that he was in the upper bunk and cheerfully jumped out and broke both his legs. He had no liking for heights and up there he seemed to be in another world. As he looked up he saw the rafters and the cracks in the bare wood. There was a little shelf, and he put his writing paper, his bottle of ink, and his shaving and washing kit on it. He had begun to shave; not that he really needed to shave every day, in fact he had been warned; 'Don't shave too soon or your beard will grow hard and bristly and you will regret it later.' But he wanted a stiff, bristly beard and so he shaved at least once every three days now.

The other lads were coming in from work. They looked dirty and tired and did not take very much notice of the new intake at first. They just took off the brown jackets, took a towel and soap and made their way to the ablutions hut. It had a long wooden shelf with metal bowls on it and a row of cold water taps. In the evenings there was hot water which was provided from a little boiler in an annexe outside the washroom. Later they met the old hands in the recreation hut and by that time they were a bit more interested in them.

'Where are you from?'

'Hostel in Ramsgate which has just folded.'

'What is it like here?'

'Awful, they pay you a few pence and they make you work all hours and they run a huge farm on our labour. It's slave labour, and when they have worn us out they will send us to Australia. That's where they used to send the criminals and now it's us. The English boys are the end, watch out for them. They are criminals and they hate us because we beat them at football last week. They are stupid and dirty and they try to get us into trouble. We have a charge-hand, he tells us what to do; he is a bit older and no better than us, but he can get you into trouble if he reports you. They take away your pocket money if you do anything wrong and the food is pure shit; we spend all our money in the canteen and the canteen is run by the camp, so they starve us, and then take away all the money we earn when we buy food there. There are no girls anywhere. It really is a shitty dump, this.'

Karl felt frightened and bewildered.

'You can hear, can't you,' said Martin, 'it's the Viennese who are doing all the moaning, they never stop complaining. It's just because they have to do some real work.'

Karl talked to another lad, Hans, who came from Leipzig, and he did not tell a very different story. 'I'll tell you what really gets me about this place. In Germany they put me into Dachau before I came away. It was just the same, the wooden huts and the barbed wire. Did you notice the barbed wire?'

Karl asked if it had been as awful in Dachau.

'No, worse. It is better here. There is hot water and there is enough food to eat and no one beats you. It isn't that I mean. It is just that everything reminds me of the place, the smell and the feeling that you can never do what you want to do – and who wants to be a farmer? It's stupid work, good enough for morons like the English boys; they are the end, absolute morons with no standards at all. They are the dregs of society and we have to work with them. They shout names at us and I can't understand what they are saying; they speak some dreadful criminal slang. This afternoon one of them called me a "biship". Do you know that one?' Karl asked if he meant bugger? 'No, I know that; no, it was more like "biship" and I am damned if I know what he was getting at. I was going to be a medical student; I had already taken my pre-med exams and now this. This place really is the end.'

Karl liked Hans. It seemed to him that despite all the complaints he was coping with the situation. He told Karl what he should do. 'Get into the cowsheds as soon as you can. That is the most interesting work and cows are nice to be with. You start off with all the stupid work but if you do it well they move you on.'

They were getting ready for the first night in the camp when an older man walked over. 'Can I see all the new lads from Ramsgate,' he barked. 'Over here!'

They trooped over and he introduced himself. 'I am Captain Rajik. I am in charge of the hut and I supervise some of you for your work groups.'

He had an Austrian accent, a square red face and he was not very tall, but he held himself quite straight, in complete contrast to all around him who had their hands in their pockets and were only half-dressed. 'Report to me tomorrow and I will sort out where you work. I want this hut to be the best hut in the camp; the beds must be square, blankets folded and everything must be tidy. Right! Get to bed and lights out in ten minutes.'

'Ai waih,' said Sigi, 'a Jewish captain; just what was lacking in our lives, I expect it is going to be just like the army here. We might as well join up, if only they would have us.'

When the lights went out the farting began; loud, huge farts and they all giggled and cheered or called to someone they knew. 'Stop it, Martin,' Karl called, 'I can tell it's you.'

'Oh, shut up you infantile idiot,' Martin called back, 'for God's sake grow up.'

There were more farts, shouts of laughter and angry calls of 'Get to sleep we've work to do in the morning,' and so they settled down to sleep.

In the morning Karl put on his new breeches; they were stiff and the shirt was scratchy and there was a fusty smell on the clothes; the jacket had certainly belonged to someone before him but the boots were new and he did not think he would ever get used to them. He envied the 'old hands' who looked comfortable in their work clothes and who seemed to know exactly what to do. They went to the dining hall and Karl received a slab of grey porridge, a hard boiled egg and as many slices of bread and marge as he wanted. The porridge had sugar on it, but not very much, and Karl and the other boys just could not eat it. 'You will when you get hungry,' one of the veterans said, grinning at their disgust. Karl made himself a sandwich out of the egg and slices of bread and washed it down with sweet tea. 'They put bromide in the tea. Supposed to stop you wanking. Doesn't seem to stop old Feingold there.' He pointed to an embarrassed looking youth, his face covered with acne spots, hair looking very dank and greasy. 'He works in the boiler house, that's why he's wearing overalls; he really is disgusting. He doesn't have to fold his sheets, he just stands them in a corner; they are so starchy, they would break if you folded them. All right?' he shouted at Feingold, 'Had a good night? How many times did you manage?'

Feingold gave a big grin, showed three fingers and seemed delighted that his existence had been recognised. Karl thought, 'Oh God, what are they going to say about me if they find out and do you get to look like Feingold if you do it as often as that?' And he felt very subdued.

Rajik called them again. 'I'll show you how to do the beds, but I only show you once. Make a real effort. If you take a pride in your room you will show the English what we can do. We must show that we are smart. We beat them at football last week. All you do is to make the straw sacks look square, pat them with pieces of wood or something to square out the corners, and then you fold the blankets like this . . .' and he did it all without much effort. But when Karl tried it was not the same and however much he patted and poked his mattress it looked uneven, nor was it any help that he had either to stand on the bed of the lad under him, and that drew angry growls, or take little jumps and come down before he had done anything very effective. Rajik looked at his efforts and said, 'You will have to improve on that, that is just a pile of rubbish.' Then he went from bed to bed saying something discouraging to each one, then he called them together and told them that the next day a better effort would be expected. Sigi told Karl, 'They say that he was in the Austro-Hungarian cavalry and that he got thrown out when Hitler came. Just imagine a Yiddisher boychik in the Austro-Hungarian cavalry,' and he fell about laughing.

Outside the boys were told to form a single rank and then they were taken to where they were going to work. 'You start on potatoes,' said the instructor, another refugee. The potato harvest was in full swing and boys with horse carts were arriving and dumping sacks of potatoes; Karl and his little gang stood by the sorting machine. A big wheel had to be turned and the potatoes fell through wire nets of varying sizes. There were three grades: big, medium and pig potatoes. The big and medium ones were going to be stored in clamps, so when a sack was full it had to be taken to one of two clamps. When enough potatoes had been piled up they were covered with straw and earth was shovelled on top. There wasn't an awful lot to do because there were so many of them. Karl turned the sorting machine handle for a time; then he took a turn at the end where the potatoes came out and put the sacks into three different heaps.

The instructor stood about, nagging at them to do it right and looking over his shoulder to see if anyone senior was coming.

For lunch they were marched to the dining hall again. There was rosy pink sausage meat hiding under a thick layer of potatoes and there was cabbage and thick brown gravy, and pudding the like of which Karl had never seen before. It was called chocolate sponge and it had custard with it.

'What shitty, mucky food,' said Sigi, and Karl was inclined to agree.

'Perhaps it is what the English eat so we might as well get used to it.'

'I'll never get used to that rubbish,' said Sigi, eating quite vigorously. 'Do you remember when we had liver and rice in paprika sauce in Ramsgate? That was decent food and you always got seconds.'

Karl met Martin and Ernst outside. They looked hot and tired. They had been picking potatoes and Karl told them what he did with their harvest. 'I thought we were supposed to learn about farming,' said Martin. 'What we did this morning I could learn in two minutes, it's deadly boring.' Karl agreed. Turning a handle on a potato sorter was not a skilled occupation, either, but he repeated Hans' advice about sticking to the work and getting to the skilled jobs more quickly. They discussed the military gent, Captain Rajik. 'Have you seen his coat?' asked Martin. 'It has a little Persian lamb collar on it; it is a sort of bum freezer and he wears it like a uniform.'

There was a medical inspection for the new boys. The doctor was another refugee; he was bald except for some back hair which stuck out in all directions.

'What is your name?'

'Hartland.'

'Not the Hartlands from Essen?'

Karl suspected that the doctor meant the other Hartlands but saw no reason why he should not cash in on their fame.

'Oh, what are we all coming to?' sighed the doctor. 'A Hartland in this ghastly place. Sit down. I tell you I don't want to be here either. There is nowhere else to go and they won't let me practise. Here I am a sort of superior nurse, and I did my training under Wolfsheim in Bonn. At least we have a little bungalow here and my daughters will go to school before long.'

In the evenings the boys sat in the recreation hut, which was bare except for benches and tables, and a wireless on a shelf high above everyone. Karl played chess, wrote letters and talked to people. He heard more about the various jobs, what was thought to be a soft option and what was hard and which instructors were slave drivers and which were reasonable. Karl wrote to Margot and told her he was not happy, and that learning to farm was not really the purpose of the place. It was just to keep them busy and the food was starchy, so starchy that he was terribly constipated, which was just as well as the lavatories were grimy. And he had been on the potato clamps for a week and he did not know what would happen the week after. It might be pigs if he was lucky.

Martin approached Karl. He was forming a group for religious boys, would he care to join? They could say morning and evening prayers together and they could see the sabbath in.

'I can't be bothered,' Karl said. 'I have had enough to do all day and I don't see the point in praying at all. It does not seem to have done you or me much good.'

Martin was deeply offended and pointed out that the place wasn't really all that bad, and he ought to have a bit of faith and courage. Karl realised that this was the end of the shared food parcels and liver sausage from the kind aunts, but he could not face anything like a prayer group. He preferred to be with Hans who told him about the human body and how it functioned. Karl now thought that he wanted to be a doctor, to be able to help people and to diagnose illness and to bandage up wounds.

It became one of his best daydreams at the sorting machine handle.

The second week came and he was still turning the handle and becoming really bored with it. Even pulling the sacks to the clamp or emptying sacks on the clamp was boring. The boys fooled around a lot, throwing potatoes at each other and taunting the instructor, who only seemed to have one worry and that was that someone in authority would see him completely out of control. 'Come on, lads,' he would plead, 'do a bit more, we must shift this pile before the next load comes.' In fact the loads of picked potatoes came over slowly because a similar state of anarchy prevailed on the potato patch. 'Look out, here comes Rajik,' someone would mutter, and they would all turn to their tasks.

Rajik strolled over looking like a man with an important mission. 'I want three boys to help me with some pipes,' he rasped, and pointed to Karl and two others. They walked over to another field higher up a hill where a drain was being dug. 'Pick up the pipes, one each, and put them into the ditch,' he commanded. Karl looked at a long line of ceramic drain pipes. He was still feeling a bit giggly after his encounter with the instructor who had pleaded with them to work, and he did not very much want to lift up any drain pipes. He bent down and said, 'They are frozen to the ground. I can't possibly pick them up.' Rajik's face, which was rather red and weather-beaten, went quite purple. 'Not pick them up?' He bent down and with his leather-gloved hand he picked up a pipe and let it drop again; then as he stood up he smacked Karl across the face. 'Frozen to the ground, eh?' Up went another pipe and Karl got another smack, this time with the outside of the glove, and Rajik went on to the next pipe. 'What do you mean, can't pick them up?' Another smack with the inside of the glove, and so he went on, along six pipes. Karl's eyes were watering but he was crying with rage rather than pain; he put his head down and butted the captain in the chest and in doing so, he covered the beautiful persian lamb collared coat with tears and snot. 'Get that lazy lout off me,' shouted the captain, 'this will have to be reported; this is insubordination which is not tolerated here,' and he walked away in a great rage.

Karl was angry, sobbing, and his cheeks were stinging. Rajik had not hit him all that hard but Karl felt humiliated and all his anger at being in the farm camp at all welled up in him. The other two told him to shut up. 'If he really reports you, you are in dead trouble. When the English lads get into real trouble they are taken to the commandant's office, held over a table and beaten with leather straps.'

Karl appealed to them. 'You can testify for me, I really hadn't done anything wrong and he just went for me. It wasn't my fault the pipes were stuck to the ground.'

'Yes, but you shouldn't have gone for him, you mustn't go for staff in the camp.'

Karl was quite frightened by now and saw himself stretched across a deal table with a gag in his mouth. It would be like in *Mutiny in the Bounty* where they poured salt water over the man's back.

In the evening he talked to Hans and Hans said, 'If you haven't heard anything by now I doubt if you will hear any more. Rajik has got a temper. He may not report you because he will have to explain how it came about that you went for him.'

That made sense but Karl felt unhappy and uneasy. He was still raging at being hit, but several boys came up to him and said, 'We hear you had a go at that shit, Rajik. Well done, did you duff him in properly?'

Karl had to admit rather feebly that no, he hadn't duffed him in, he had just butted him in the chest. 'But he had snot all over his coat,' he added proudly.

Martin came up sounding slightly annoyed. 'I hear you have been getting into trouble. Really someone with a good family background like yours should not allow himself to be provoked like that. Treat people like Rajik with contempt and keep them at a distance. He would hate that much more than being attacked. Come to the canteen.'

Karl had a few pence and had not been near the canteen yet. Outside the hut Martin put his arm round him and said, 'You really are getting into bad company, you must watch it here. The place is full of people who are just waiting to take sexual advantage of a young chap like you.' Karl wished he had not got his arm round his shoulder quite so tightly and felt uncomfortable. He wondered to himself what Martin was up to, and wriggled his way out of his clasp.

'It is just that you have got such nice fair hair and a complexion like a girl. There are people who would easily take advantage of you, so you had better look out. At least I have warned you.'

They had reached the canteen which was in the main building of the compound, and a girl was serving. Karl noticed that she was pretty but had no breasts worth noticing and he thought that was a great pity. He bought a tube of Smarties; he had read the advertisements in *Picture Post* which said they were supposed to stop one from fiddling and twitching. Martin bought a bar of Aero chococlate and carefully broke off one piece for Karl. 'Are you sure about the prayer meetings?' he asked, and Karl felt guilty but said, 'No, thank you.'

'At least allow me to bless you in that case.' And Martin put his hands on Karl's head and started muttering in Hebrew and Karl just wished he would leave him alone. They went back into the hut and someone teased Karl. 'What have you been up to? You look all pink and flushed.'

There was a fight going on in the dormitory. 'Wanker' Feingold was being pushed and slapped around by Spier. Spier was the senior lad, the 'Big Daddy' in the place. What he said went and no one argued with him. He didn't usually take advantage of his senior position and Karl admired his confidence and weighty authority. Spier was so angry that he hit Feingold who fell backwards over a bed. His nose was bleeding and he had a silly, embarrassed smile. 'We don't want any of your filthy tricks here; understand? I am going to kick you up the arse until your teeth come marching out if you don't stop your filth.'

Karl was terrified and thought to himself, 'What will they do to me if they ever catch me at it?' But it appeared that Feingold had been pinching things. He had quite a store under his bed and now Spier was dealing with the matter.

Sigi was excited by the fight. 'Did you see that? Spier was dealing with Feingold. He had it coming to him, the dirty wanker. I mean we all do it but not like him. He thinks he is special just because he has got a cushy number in the boiler house and because they have issued him with a boiler suit. This is what we used to sing in Vienna when there was a street fight:

> *If it comes to a scrap*
> *Beat out the crap*
> *stick your knife in to the hilt*
> *and make the bastard wilt.*

He kept singing that song all evening, looking across to Karl as if they were both in a conspiracy together. Karl decided to have a fight with someone, too, so that he would be respected.

The occasion came on the potato sorting machine. There was a lad every one disliked. He hated the work even more than the others and sometimes just would not help. 'Give me a hand with the potatoes, David,' Karl asked. He had to drag the big potatoes to the clamp and thought it would be easier if two pulled at the sack. David said, 'You are not an instructor, you can't give me orders, do it yourself.' Karl felt all excited, this was his chance, he knew that no one would support David, and while David was not all that small he certainly wasn't stronger than Karl. 'I'll give you a thick ear if you won't help me.'

'You and who else, you can't do anything, you are just a huge arsehole.'

This, as far as Karl was concerned, was fighting talk and he squared up to David in the way Mr Charc had taught him. Right shoulder forward, feet well apart, he tapped his face with his left hand to get the range right and then punched with his right and hit David between the teeth and nose. David fell down but Karl nearly screamed with pain. In films, bare fists always crash into faces, the opponent falls down and the victor walks away triumphant, but Karl was writhing in pain and was sure he had broken his hand. David was lying on the ground, crying and his nose was bleeding a bit.

The instructor turned on them in a great panic. 'What do you think you are at, we can't have you fighting here; get on with the work, I am going to put you on report, Karl.'

They all went on with turning the sorting machine handle and dragging the sacks. David was blubbing quietly and Karl was not far from it either. His hand hurt and he felt all trembly and worried about the report.

In the evening Sigi was impressed. 'That's what you need to do in a place like this. You have got to show that no one can push you around and if you have a fight they can see you can take care of yourself, anyhow that schmuck had it coming to him.'

Karl said he was worried about the report, but Sigi said, 'What can they do to you? Stick you in an approved school?'

Hans looked at Karl's hand and told him it wasn't broken. 'Look, you can still grasp things, just have a plaster put on over the cut. You are getting a fine reputation for yourself, aren't you, first that to-do with Rajik, now the boy. What are you trying to prove? You must try and be a bit more civilised. Don't get taken over by the things that are worst here.'

Karl felt ashamed and then the next day was delighted to be told that he could go with Hans to get in the kale.

'It will make a change for you,' said Hans. 'Mind you, you have to get up at five,' but Karl did not really mind that.

He put his towel over the end of the bed to show he wanted an early call, and when it came got dressed as quietly as he could, then joined Hans and they took a horse and cart into the kale field. It was quite dark when they set out and they walked slowly.

'Did you know,' said Hans, 'Freud has died.'

'Who is Freud?' asked Karl.

'God, where did you live? Never heard of Freud? He was a great psychiatrist and he discovered the unconscious.'

'What is the unconscious?'

'It is the part of the mind that lacks control. You do things because your reason tells you to do them, and then there is another force that makes you do things you don't really want to do. What seems like a mistake at first is really your unconscious mind at work. He was a Jew, but he did not believe in religion any more. He was expelled from Vienna and came to England. He really is one of the most famous men in this century.'

Karl was deeply intrigued and wanted to know more. 'Can I read about his work?'

'Yes, he has written a lot but I haven't got anything here. Let's see if we can get some books.'

They walked into the kale field and cut the plants with a bill-hook. Every time Karl cut, a shower of drops fell all over him, and soon he was wet all over.

'Next time, tie a sack round you,' said Hans. When they had filled the cart they went back. For the first time Karl realised that this was a very beautiful place. The hills were gentle, there were hedges and the early sun made everything look golden. It was a cold, bare morning and yet he felt that things were going to grow around him, and the beauty of it all moved him but he could not talk to anyone about it. There was a second session of breakfast for the lads who worked with the cows or had other tasks that made them get up early. Karl felt he had moved up in the world. He was now with much older and more serious young men and they seemed more measured in the way they carried on. The conversation at the table was mainly about how they could get out of the place, but no one had any very good ideas. 'We could join the army, but they don't want us. It seems ridiculous. Here is a country at war with the Germans, here is a group of us who hate the National Socialists and who are prepared to fight and they won't even look at us.'

It became very cold and the cold made everyone miserable. There were pipe stoves at each end of the huts which were fed with coke. It was nice and warm within two feet of the stove but the hut as a whole was still cold. There was only one thickness of planks and there were many cracks in the walls. Karl stuffed pieces of paper into the cracks above his bed but it did not make much difference. Going to bed meant for him changing clothes rather than undressing. He put his work clothes under the blanket and in the morning they were reasonably warm. Unfortunately he could not do that with his boots and they became stiff and difficult to put on after a night of frost. Bed-making worried Karl less than at the beginning. He had found some cardboard boxes behind the kitchen, torn them into long strips and stuffed these into the straw mattress. This made it look all nice and square. He put his night clothes under the mattress and he was able to fold the blankets much more easily. There was a good deal of coughing at night, more coughing than farting even, and Sigi coughed the most. Karl told him to report sick and Sigi went to the refugee doctor in the evening after work.

'You have got a temperature and you will have to go to the sanatorium. Will you take him, Hartland?'

Karl walked to the sanatorium with Sigi. It was a separate brick building with a large oak door. Karl rang the bell, the door was opened, but only a little bit. 'What do you want?'

'I have brought my friend from the camp, the doctor says he is ill.'

'What doctor? There is no doctor there. I am not having that man telling me what to do.'

Karl was beginning to feel angry and he was not at all sure that he had understood everything correctly, but he persevered. 'He is very ill, can you look at him? He has a temperature.'

Karl put his foot into the door and began to push it open and before long he and Sigi were standing in the hall. The place reeked of some disinfectant and the floor was polished to a degree of shininess Karl had never seen before. There was a hospital ward behind the little hall and a narrow piece of carpet went down the middle of the ward. The matron looked really cross and kept on saying 'awkward' a word Karl did not know. As always when he heard a new word he would repeat it to himself and store it up in his mind until he could reach his dictionary. She felt Sigi's forehead, said something about 'awkward' and let him stay.

Before long Karl was coughing too. It was worst at night and others would shout at him because he was disturbing their sleep. He reported sick and was sent to the sanatorium where he found himself in a bed next to Sigi.

'It's fantastic here,' Sigi said, 'sheets, and you can sleep all day and it's warm. I should be here for at least a fortnight if I work it right.'

Sigi was in fact sent back to the camp the next day. 'See you soon,' he said cheerfully.

There were English boys in the ward and they were looked ofter by a strange boy with a long, thin red nose – everyone in the camp seemed not only to have red noses but the area under the nose and round it was inflamed as well – and he had very short cropped red hair. He could move his lower lip right over the tip of his nose because he had no teeth in his mouth, and if Karl looked at him closely he could see that he was much older than most of the lads. He would mop over the perfect floor in the morning using the broom as a drum major used his baton. He jumped over it, balanced it on his chin, swivelled it over his back and then caught it perfectly. He took Karl's lunch tray away and piled all sorts of crockery on it and then he crossed his legs, sat down, rose again and, to round off the entertainment, let off a huge fart. Karl thought it was funny but it became clear that these rituals happened after every meal; it was his skill and he was proud of it.

There was very little communication between the refugees and the English boys. As Martin had put it, 'They all speak some dreadful slang, probably Cockney, and we must be careful not to learn to speak like that. The English despise slang like Cockney; we must learn the proper Oxford accent.' Karl did not discover what the proper Oxford accent was, and the only word he could pick up from the lads was 'fucking' because they said that all the time. One of the patients called him a 'bloody, fucking foreign bastard' and Karl understood the meaning of that quite well. He, too, was discharged after a few days, coughing still, but not quite so badly and he was given a bottle of linctus to take if the cough got too bad at night.

Christmas came and depressed them immensely. The recreation hut was decorated with a few streamers and on Christmas day a member of staff came in dressed up as Father Christmas and they all got a present. Karl was given a little diary and a blue handkerchief with white dots and they sang Christian carols, being too polite to say that really Jews had a different festival. It was clear that the camp staff were trying to be nice to them. The Christmas dinner was fat pork, brown gravy, a lump of apple sauce which was very sour, a roast potato, brussel sprouts which were quite cold and, horror of horror, a dark brown pudding over which they poured a yellow custard flavoured with rum. 'God,' said Sigi, 'it's worse when they try to cook well than when they do the ordinary rubbish they give us.' There was a cracker and they all sat there terribly embarrassed and not feeling in the least like any kind of festivity. They talked about roast goose and red cabbage, Sachertorte and cheese cake and the next day Karl went back to cutting kale early in the morning.

One day, suddenly, in February he was called into the office. 'You have been admitted to a school in Elmfield and will leave here tomorrow. Pack your things. We will get you a ticket and you will go to Elmfield on the train.'

This was the first Karl had heard about a school. His sister was still working in Elmfield as a maid servant and his miserable letters had moved her into action. She had donned her best grey costume, put on her fur and had requested an interview with the headmaster. She asked him if he would take her brother who was miserable in the approved school camp, and asked how much the fees were. She had also written to the other Hartlands in New York, and they agreed to pay the fees, but she had not told Karl earlier because she thought he would become even more demoralised if the plan did not work. Karl did not know what a grammar school was, he did not know where Elmfield was, but he knew he could leave the camp and that was good enough for him. 'Hand in your work clothes this evening and one of the instructors will take you to the store room.'

It did not take Karl long to pack. He put on his best brown sports jacket, a silk tie and grey trousers and thought he looked quite English like that. His farewells were quick. 'Good luck and don't get into too many fights.'

'You are a lucky sod getting out like that, I wish someone would do that for me.'

Martin said, 'This is a fantastic opportunity for you. Make the most of it. See you one day.'

Karl was scared that he might start blessing him again but the thought did not seem to occur to Martin. Hans said, 'Now you have a chance to get to a medical school. I expect I will get there too, one day.'

Karl was taken to the station with his huge brown and smaller black case and stood there clutching his ticket for Elmfield via Reading.

Chapter 11

Karl got to the station in Elmfield in a state of confusion. He had held his ticket up to people and had said, 'Please', and they had pointed him in the right direction to the right trains and, amazingly, in the afternoon he arrived. He said 'Grammar School' to the guard, who pointed down the hill and said it was a long way. Karl did not dare to leave suitcases so he dragged them along. 'Omnia mea mecum porto' his father would no doubt have said at that point, and Karl grinned to himself, but it was terribly cold and the cases were heavy. He went past a frozen pond and boys were sliding on it. They must belong to the school he said to himself. They wore brown cloth caps with a yellow spot the size of a fried egg o1 top and they had enormous scarves which fluttered behind them as they slid on the ice. He watched for some time while he had a rest and then he dragged himself on again. Suddenly he heard Margot call him. 'Karl, baby bunny rabbit, over here.' She came rushing out of a terraced house and said, 'We have been expecting you, these are the Barts, they are from Vienna, their boy is at the school, I am so glad I saw you, I had no idea when you would come.'

Karl was taken into Margot's friends' house and sat down at a table where tea was served; there was bread, butter and corned beef.

'You look so thin and pale, was it a dreadful place? Never mind the school is nice, I like the headmaster and there are several refugee boys there.'

Karl just sat, hardly believing that he had got there at all, that there was food and that he had met his sister almost by accident. Mrs Bart said, 'Eat. There is plenty. My boy is doing his homework at school and he won't be back till later, but he likes it there. They are very nice to the refugee boys, specially the headmaster and his wife.'

Karl wanted to know so many things but they would not have known the answers. What was he going to do, knowing hardly any English? He had not been inside a school for nearly three years, he had done no school work except English lessons at Ramsgate. He could, with the help of a dictionary, just about read and understand *Picture Post* but ordinary conversation was very difficult.

'What is your son's English like?'

'Oh marvellous, he speaks better than any of us, just a few weeks and you will talk just like the rest of the boys there. Eat some more, have some more tea, you must be starving.'

She turned to Margot and said, 'He does look thin and grey.'

Karl explained that he had just had a cough and had got over it.

'Funny,' Margot said, 'he used to be so fat, and now he is thin; I think I preferred him fat.' Karl, whose daydreams had always been that he would be slim and of trim figure was amazed. He did not know he had got thin. At the camp there were only small shaving mirrors and he had not really seen himself for a long time. They asked him about the camp and said it was dreadful, but what could one do? These were difficult times and they supposed they had nowhere else to put the boys. Margot then walked with Karl to the school. 'I'll introduce you to the headmaster and then I have got to be back at the house. Listen; about the money. The other Hartlands have said they will pay the fees but be careful. They aren't very keen and there must not be too many extras. If you need any school clothes you get them from Matron, or at least she will see that you get things and they are then put on the bill.'

Karl felt depressed. He did not know how he could or could not spend money, but he realised that a promise to pay the fees had not been easy to get and that the money might be withheld; then where would he go?

They reached the school. It was dark and Karl could not see very much. A maid answered the doorbell and Karl and Margot were shown into a huge drawing room. The room made a tremendous impact on Karl. The walls were all painted white. There was a big carved white marble fireplace and logs were burning in it; the carpet was white and the furniture was in a modern style that Karl had not seen before. At his home in Essen it had all been mock Chippendale, mock Renaissance and mock Regency; here was a style all of its own and it was all white. He was scared he would make something dirty. In part he was still in the camp where there had only been bare pine planks, corrugated iron, and mud outside.

The man in the room came forward and said, 'I am Mr Steven, the headmaster here, this is my wife, Vanessa.'

They smiled at Karl. He felt frightened; it had been a long time since grown-up people had smiled at him in that way. This seemed just open friendliness and he felt he must be on his guard. They were given tea and very thin little sandwiches and funny cakes and Karl sat on the edge of the chair trying very hard to understand what was said. There was something about staying with the Edwards, boys would show him, then Margot said she had to get back and went away.

When Karl came out of the drawing room several boys were standing around his suitcases. They all wore grey suits, had grey pullovers and ties with brown and yellow stripes. The hall furniture was made entirely out of carved wood, there were two large sideboards and a carpet at the bottom of the stairs. A carpet, Karl thought with amazement and pleasure. The headmaster said something and a boy was fetched. 'This is Karl Hartland and this is Harry Pring.' Karl looked at a thin, sharp featured boy who had spotty skin but was something of a smart dresser, because his tie stuck out almost at right angles until it went into his pullover where it was kept in place with a pin.

'Take him into supper and then to the Edwards.'

So Karl was led by the arm into the evening meal. The dining room was huge with thick, wooden tables, and the water was in brown earthenware jugs. Most of the boys seemed to have special jars and pots of jam which they had brought into the meal and they were served bread and tea and some jam. The boys around him seemed friendly, but Karl could not understand what they said and he just smiled and shrugged his shoulders. After a time they gave up and ignored him and just talked to each other.

Harry then waved him on. 'Take you to Matron first.' He gave a conspiratorial wink and said 'crackle' and in case Karl had not understood that this was important he repeated 'crackle' and laughed and laughed. He pushed Karl into a room and Karl nearly gave a shriek of horror. There sat a lady under a green glass lamp shade; she wore a thickly starched overall and she had bright red hair that was done up in a bun and had steel clips through it, her eyebrows were invisible and her face seemed covered with rice powder or something very white. She looked up and did not smile, just said, 'You are a new boy? Come tomorrow and I'll give you chits for the school shop. Take him, Pring.' Harry Pring advanced obediently and pulled Karl out of the room, almost bowing with respect as they went out.

They went to the Edwards' house; a fifteen minute walk in complete darkness. At the end of the road was a small, detached, pebble dash house. They went round the back into the kitchen, Harry put on slippers that were waiting for him and led Karl into a room with a comfortable chair and a big coal fire blazing in the grate. Mr Edwards was an English teacher at the school. He was a small, grey haired man, with hair parted in the middle, strong features that seemed carved out of wood, a big forward sticking chin and bushy eyebrows. He introduced himself and his wife, a small woman in a wine-coloured house coat and slippers. She usually had two or three boys from the school as boarders she explained to Karl, then smiled at him, told him to sit down and gave him a cup of cocoa. Presently another boy came in. 'This is Derek; he is a school prefect already.' Karl could tell that he was a higher rank than Harry. He wore a buttoned waistcoat and in his hand was a brown cap that had a golden tassel hanging from it. Karl was fascinated by the cap and told himself that at all costs he must get one of those. He was shown the room he was sharing with Harry. He had a bed, a real, soft bed with sheets and blankets, a chest of drawers and part of the wardrobe to himself. Karl fell asleep confused, anxious and hoping that things would work out. There seemed to be nothing further he could do.

Breakfast surprised Karl. There were dainty triangles of toast, half a grilled tomato each and each boy had a piece of butter with a little flag stuck in it with his name on it. After the huge chunks of bread and marge Karl was amazed at such daintiness and he tried to eat slowly and nicely to show that he knew how to behave in a refined environment. Harry and Derek walked him to the school where he was handed over to another boy who was to take him round. Prayers first. Karl was led into a hall built in the Greek style. There was a First World War memorial with *dulce et decorum est pro patria mori* on it. Karl remembered that the identical phrase had appeared on the Goethe Gymnasium War Memorial. The boys were each given a hymn book and older boys went around hitting the smaller ones on the head with their hymn books. It seemed that talking was not allowed. The masters filed in, each one in a huge billowing black gown. Karl was nudged into opening his hymn book at the right place but after that everything was incomprehensible. The headmaster spoke to the school, it was clear he was not pleased about something; and then Karl was led into his classroom. He was, it seemed from the Latin letters on the exercise books in the fourth form, which would correspond to the form he had left in Essen. The lesson was maths with a master who looked pink and drew things elegantly on the board which the boys copied. He walked over to Karl, gave him a pencil and a piece of paper and Karl copied the things from the board and then the man said 'good'. It was Latin after that and Karl at last understood something that was going on; it seemed to him that the Latin done here was easier than the Latin in

Germany but the pronunciation was different. This time the teacher had a walrus moustache, a florid face and rather elegant clothes. Karl noticed his rough woven tie with envy and admiration. The pace of the lessons seemed leisurely; one boy turned round and gave Karl a huge wink and then when the master asked him a question he said, 'Wait a minute, I knew it yesterday, hang on,' and the master waited. Karl was deeply astonished and remembered his lessons with Ivan the Terrible who gave one a four if one did not stand to attention and shout the correct answer out in a crisp military tone. Karl was pulled from lesson to lesson until a boy put his fingers up to his mouth and stuffed them in to indicate food. Karl smiled and nodded and followed him into lunch. He sat next to a huge man with a large Roman nose, curly hair and the most fascinating twitches; first he would bring his hand to this throat, then he would rub it down the front of his pullover several times and then his forehead would twitch. He said, 'Hmm! Come here, Karl.' The way he said 'Karl' made Karl realise that he spoke German, but that was all the German he heard from him. He sat Karl next to him and distributed the food, muttering 'hm' and calling boys by their first names. It was clear that he liked some more than others. Suddenly he was angry, shouting at one little boy at the end of the table, 'Over there! Stand against the wall.' The child crept out of his place and stood against the light blue wall, soon to be joined by others who had offended in some way. It was scaring for Karl to see the sudden shift of mood, 'Hm, Karl, some more?' and a ladle of brown stew descended on his plate. 'More' was obviously important, and the boys sitting next to him got more but not the ones at the end of the table who looked envious. The same procedure over the pudding, some announcements and then Harry took Karl over.

'No games for you yet, go and see Crackle for your things from the school shop.' Karl was given chits. At first he thought they said shits, but he understood when he saw the numbered sheets out of an order book. One chit for a tie, another for a cap, another for a scarf and one for football boots. Karl was horrified in case these things cost a lot of money, but liked the idea of having the same uniform as the other boys. He did not have a grey flannel suit but Matron said, 'You'd better wear out what you have got at the moment.' Harry and Karl trooped into the town and went into an ancient looking shop where Harry adopted a very regal tone. 'School uniform for this new boy, please.'

An old man with a tape measure round his neck found all the things, which were kept in dusty looking boxes. When he had finished he kept the chits.

'Got any money?' asked Harry.

Karl said, 'No.'

'Bad luck,' said Harry and went into a sweet shop and came out with several pieces of chocolate which he ate happily with Karl walking by his side. Harry clearly found Karl boring as he could not talk to him; he made some attempts, but Karl could not cope with the fast flow of information nor with Harry's vocabulary. He had names Karl did not recognise for everyone. The eccentric man at lunch appeared to be called 'Toss', the classics master 'Jacko', and Harry referred to the Edwards as the 'Little Teds'. Karl was shown the library and an elegantly drawling youth came up. 'You are from Germany, I hear. I came from Vienna, my name is Joseph. I hear you are an oppidan.'

Karl knew what an oppidan was, one who lived outside the town walls. Clearly he lived outside the school and that made him an oppidan. He hoped the boy from Vienna would talk to him in German but he would not. Karl wanted to show that he was a man of culture and education and so at random he picked *Nicholas Nickleby* from the shelf and sat with it in front of him.

'Ah, Dickens,' Joseph said, 'very good, you will be all right here.'

The next day Karl visited Margot at the house where she was a maid. He went to the front door and rang the bell. An elderly lady came out and said, 'Not this door, come round to the side.' She re-appeared and said 'That's better' when Karl went through the door. Margot introduced him to the lady and said 'That's nanny'. She showed Karl round the house and

Karl thought her room in the attic pretty grim. There were just two beds, some hooks and a chest of drawers. Margot gave him some cake and tea and they went for a walk. There were pine forests and they walked up a hill until they had a magnificent view. Margot said, 'I have given them my notice; I am leaving and taking a job in a house in Godalming; that's only ten miles from here. I can't stand these people any more, they are mean and they despise us and the nanny spies on us and reports everything we do. I'll see if it is better in Godalming. In any case, you don't want to be in a school where it is known that your sister is a skivvy in the same town.'

Karl felt sad, he enjoyed talking German to Margot. It was to him as if he had not talked to any one for days, but Margot said, '*and* you will learn to speak English much better if I am not around.'

Gradually, as if a fog was clearing, Karl began to understand more of what was said to him. What he said was understood by others, he was able to tell people apart and he learnt who was powerful and who was not. In the first place there were the prefects. They were older boys and Karl was impressed with their mature ways, their pipes and slightly different clothes. They had a study on the top floor. He was not allowed inside but it was full of smoke, plates with half eaten pieces of toast and shelves full of textbooks. Karl was older and bigger than many of the boys in his form and he was difficult to place. Another problem was his complete ignorance of games. He had played football with his class in Essen but again it had been an occasion when everyone shouted at him, told him to get a move on and that he was useless. Harry could not understand that anyone was not keen on games; he was in the first eleven for football and cricket and that gave him a certain advantage over Derek who was a school prefect, but had very little authority over Harry who teased him all the time. Karl did not like Harry but depended on him for guidance. He talked another language that Karl knew he must master. 'You know that geezer over there?'

'What? Who?'

'That geezer, that guy, bloke, gink; Christ! Where have you been, don't you know anything?' He talked fast and made few concessions to Karl's ignorance. He only referred to masters by their nicknames and Karl had to learn many of them and also that every woman had a 'ma' put in front of her name, so Mrs Steven became MaSteve, the lady who ran a cake shop next to the school was MaBarnes, and Mrs Ted a double twist, MaTed.

Then there was the girls' school. A whole school had been evacuated from London. The girls had been billeted all over the little town. In the afternoons when the boys played games the girls streamed in and took over the school. Harry called them 'the dames' and it was clear that he was a great one with the dames. 'Got a girl?' he asked Karl, and Karl, feeling humiliated, said, 'No.' He did not feel like telling Harry that there had been no girls where he had been, and in any case Karl was not absolutely sure what to do with 'dames'. He just longed for girls, and when the girls cycled and walked into the school yard he stood in the bathroom behind the curtain and looked. 'We have dances with them once a term; you are lucky, there will be one at the end of the term, unless they cancel it. They always find reasons for cancelling the dances. Last time it was chicken pox. I bet it will be whooping cough this time. They don't like us to get together, but I meet this smashing dame on Sunday and we go for walks. Oh boy, oh boy. Can you dance?'

Karl could not, and Harry very nearly gave him up for hopeless. He also realised that Karl was a swot and a swot was the one thing that Harry could not stand. Karl wanted to say to him, 'Look, where I have been, it made me realise I must have an education. I don't want to spend the rest of my life turning the handle of a potato sorting machine. This is my only chance. I must work all the time.'

Karl had made up his mind that he was not going to waste time in school because wasting time cost money. He was also careful about his spending. If he had tennis lessons that would cost extra or if he had extra food like the other boys, that would cost too. He did not have milk in the evening because he did not want to increase the school bills. Margot's warning had sunk in deep; he did not want to be taken away because it was too expensive. He felt lonely but said to himself, 'If I have friends here I will waste time and if I waste time I won't learn anything.'

Homework, or rather it was called 'prep', was done in the classrooms and the session was supervised by prefects. The other boys tried to relieve the boredom by taunting the prefect if he was thought to be soft or just by creating situations that diverted the whole class. Karl tried to ignore all this and just worked on. It was difficult enough for him because the language came to him slowly and there was so much he just did not know. There were a few subjects in which he was ahead of his class, particularly Latin. Geography presented few difficulties because all he had to do was to fill in a notebook with notes that had already been dictated in class. The geography teacher, Mr Harris, had been a captain in the first war. He was quite bald but a few strands of hair went across his head like tram lines. He, too, was host to a number of 'oppidans' and Harry said that the only good thing about him and MaHarris was that they had a pretty niece staying with them. 'Fantastic blonde,' Harry said, cupping his hands under his chest and miming a sensuous swoon.

Harris embarrassed Karl by pointing to him when he talked about tweed. 'Tweed is the main cottage industry in the Shetlands; tweed looks like that,' pointing to Karl, who went puce with embarrassment. He wished he could have had a grey suit but obviously it was better to wear out the clothes he had brought with him first.

Several other refugee boys had either made themselves known to Karl or they would briefly say where they were from and then they would move on again. They wanted to merge with the other boys and not be too distinct a group. One, Heinz Nordmann, was a huge blond boy, already a school prefect, and he viewed Karl with some distaste. Ben, another boy somewhat younger than Karl, spent more time with him and explained things. 'Nordmann hates being a refugee. He was already in the

Hitler Youth and they turfed him out when they found that he was half-Jewish; watch him, he tends to pick on us.'

Ben was small, had a huge pointed nose and sniffled after every few words. Karl did not take to him but he was the only one who talked to him and explained things, and Ben's explanations were easier to understand than Harry's, and in any case Harry avoided Karl during the day and would only talk to him when they sat by the fire at the Edwards' house. Ben was in Karl's form and had been in England for a long time so he had forgotten most of his German. 'Mind you,' he said, 'that is a pity because if you know German well that is one certain subject in the school certificate examination.' He explained to Karl that at the end of the fifth year they would take this examination and it was important. 'If you do well you can go into the sixth form and then possibly to university.'

It was through Ben that Karl learnt about the English educational system. He only wished the other boys did not dislike Ben so much. Karl could not understand why they did, for although he sniffed and had a slightly supercilious air he wasn't all that bad. One reason perhaps was that Ben was the head-master's specially adopted refugee boy. The others thought that he had too close a relationship with the head and his wife and told them secrets; also he was a swot and much better at school work than a good many other boys; the staff were also suspicious of these strange boys who had come in from elsewhere and who were reputed to be 'clever'.

As Karl understood more he took part in the lessons more. He was proud when 'Old Toss' complimented him on the drawing of the alimentary canal he had done in the biology homework, but less happy when his book was held up and Toss said, 'Look at his drawing. He has only been here a few weeks and his work is better than most of you, hmpf.' In the break a red haired boy came up to him. 'I'm Tony, I'm Jewish too, you seem to be doing well here. I bet they make you a prefect soon, you are big enough.'

Karl was gratified and frightened. Becoming a prefect was his greatest secret hope but when he compared himself to the present reign of older boys he saw that he was not suitable.

'You wait,' said Tony, 'Steve is trying to change things; he wants intelligent boys as prefects, not the football louts.' From conversations at the Edwards' house Karl had begun to realise that the headmaster was a controversial figure. Harry complained bitterly about him to Mr and Mrs Edwards saying that he was full of modern ideas and that you did not know where you were with him. Harry had been at the school under Steve's predecessor, a clergyman 'of the old school, and a gentleman'. Little Ted said that he was not at all sure about all these modern ideas.

As far as Karl could judge the one modern idea Harry approved of was that Steven had abolished Matron's weekly dosing of all the boys. It appeared that the boys had had to line up in the entrance hall and each had been given a spoonful of purgative, regardless of previous performance.

Then there were the weekly house meetings. As Karl understood more of what was said around him he realised that these were something unusual. All the boys in the boarding house met on Sunday afternoon and they talked about the rules, what they wanted and how things should be run. One of the boys was chairman, another treasurer, and another secretary. Certain rules were laid down. For example, whoever spoke had first to ask permission from the chairman. Karl was enormously intrigued by these proceedings. All his life he had been told what to do; he had not always done it, but if he chose not to then the only course open to him had been either to be rebellious or sly. Grown-ups had known what was best for him and they had shunted him around from one place to another as it suited them. Here there was consultation and discussion, though not always a smooth orderly progression. Steve, on one occasion, became terribly angry with boys and said that if they went on with that line of argument – it was about visiting the cinema in town – he would withdraw the privileges he had granted.

'There you are,' said Harry, 'he doesn't really mean it, it is just a way of keeping us sweet. The moment we want something serious he gets ratty and threatens this, that and the other.'

Little Ted couldn't make up his mind which side he was on. 'Someone has got to be in charge and take the responsibility for giving orders. You can't just have an argument about everything. Take the army . . .' (he had just joined the Home Guard) . . . 'if the officers say, "take the hill," you can't sit down and have a discussion about whether to obey or not.'

MaTed joined in. 'But this isn't a matter of life and death and why shouldn't the boys know the reasons for the rules. All right, so he got angry, but at least he was there to argue and put his case and I suppose there are things a headmaster has to make up his own mind about, like going to the cinema. I think it is jolly brave of him to try this sort of thing.'

'Well, the boys don't trust him,' said Harry. 'They say he goes about asking questions and prowling round the dormitories at night. That's the prefect's job. No wonder they call him "snoop". With old Acton you got a caning and that was that. This one just talks to you, it gives you the shivers, talk, talk, talk. Mind you, I don't like the cane, it stings. Old Jacko, he still canes but not very often, doesn't half hurt when he does it.'

Karl knew he would not like to be caned. However awful the school in Germany had been they had never hit boys and he was sure that beatings were humiliating as well as painful. He remembered the incident with Rajik and how angry he had become.

Karl learnt a lot from the Teds, they argued furiously but they got on well together. Little Ted would always take what MaTed called 'a reactionary line'. He was also a great optimist and however bad the war news, and it seemed to get worse with every bulletin, he would say, 'Never mind, they have got things up their sleeve we don't know about, you will see it will turn out all right.'

'But, Gruffydd,' his wife would argue, 'where are the generals, where are the leaders? There is no inspiration, they seem to be unable to make any move ahead of the Germans.'

Little Ted would puff at his pipe and look profoundly into the future and then would jump up and make copies of poems

203

and notes for his lessons the next day. He wrote beautifully, each letter printed separately. He made notes on lives of the poets and difficult words, and explained classical allusions. He then placed the page on a jelly, and from the jelly he would print enough copies for the class. Each copy looked beautiful and Karl really could not understand why the boys treated Little Ted so badly. They laughed, made signs behind his back and the fifth formers would jostle him and push him; once the top villains in the school locked him in his own store cupboard. At home Little Ted would tell them how strict he had been and how he had once thrown a boy out of the room right against the banister. 'Oh, Gruffydd,' MaTed would wail, 'you are far too strict; you are terrible when you are angry, they are only boys.' And he would say, rather pleased with himself, 'If you don't keep them in order they will just walk over you, I know that I am fierce, but you have got to be with louts like Turner and Stone around.'

Karl knew those two and kept out of their way; they were huge and they wore their tiny school caps on the backs of their heads; their ties were always at an angle and the top buttons of their shirts were undone. They hated the school and all in authority hated them. They put out their cigarettes just before they walked into the school gate and the prefects walked the other way when they saw them. They were very good at football, and because Harry, too, was in the first eleven he had a good relationship with them. He admired them because they could do all the things he would have liked to do, and they had the freedom of being day boys. They went to their own village dances but the boarders had to wait for their dance until the last week of the term.

Karl was walking 'up town' with Harry one day; it did not happen very often because Harry did not find Karl interesting or amusing, but they joined up by accident because Karl wanted a stamp and Harry some sweets. They met a girl from the girls' school who greeted Harry as if she had not seen him for years and gave Karl a bored side glance. 'Coming to the dance?'

'Yeah, perhaps I am, and perhaps I'm not.'

Harry had a special tough way of talking and he jerked his cap back upwards. His cap had a larger peak, for cricket, to keep the sun out of his eyes, as he explained to Karl, when he noticed this further distinction in the uniform.

'Will you dance with me?'

'I may do and I may not, I will if you ask nicely.'

Karl was standing slightly behind Harry, hating the girl, hating Harry and himself. What could he say? I have just come from an approved school where they kept criminals and I have been turning the handle of a potato sorting machine? He was embarrassed because of his bad English. Every time he talked to anybody they would say, 'And where are you from?' and he would say, 'From Germany,' and they would look puzzled as if to say, 'but are we not at war with them?' And he wanted to add, 'But I am Jewish, you see, and they threw me out.' But he felt bad about telling people that he was Jewish. What did it mean to him? He had refused to join the prayer circle, he really did not know in what sense being Jewish was supposed to make him different. If, when they had pork for dinner, they said, 'But Jews aren't allowed to eat pork, are they?' he would have to say, 'But in my family we have always eaten ham and things like that.' It was all very difficult, and besides, Karl had not talked to any girls of his own age. The nearest he had come to a girl was the 'green one' in Ramsgate. So he just stood there shifting from one foot to the other and indicating that he had important things to do.

'What's the matter with you?' asked Harry, 'not interested in dames? Are you coming to the dance?'

Harry was nicer about the dance because he wanted to borrow one of Karl's beautiful silk ties. On that evening they were allowed to wear their own ties. Their preparation for the dance was most painstaking. The Edwards provided kettles of hot water for shaving, and Harry wore a hair net. They kept on tying and re-tying their ties, and when they went into Big School Karl was paralysed. He did not know how to dance, or what he was supposed to do, but he did know that he wanted to meet a girl, and there they stood in bunches. All he had to do was to walk across and ask, and then one of them might dance with him. The teachers were making attempts to mix them up. 'Come on, Paul Jones, girls in the middle, boys on the outside, everyone join in,' and Karl found himself holding on to Ann Jones, blonde, smiling and wanting to talk to him.

'Where are you from? I think it is interesting, you are different from the others, I like your foreign accent.'

Karl was enchanted, and then the Paul Jones was over and he had to go back into his corner, and he wanted to dance with Ann again, she had not even minded when he stepped on her toes.

'You liked Ann Jones,' Harry said, 'smashing girl, but you need to look out, she is Sandy's girl.'

Sandy was a tough older boy who had enormous prestige with the boys in the school. He had sardonic good looks and the girls thought they were lucky when he walked out with them. Not all the girls bothered with the schoolboys. There was Joan Coulton, 'she goes out with soldiers', and Mary Bright, 'only goes out with the son of the people she stays with'.

During the holidays the boys stayed in the school and it was quite good fun. They had the place to themselves, went for walks, and Karl read a lot. He spent more time with Ben, whom he would have liked much better if he had not been so disliked by other boys. Ben told him about his interests, he knew about Freud, he wanted to be a concert pianist and he was not a success with the girls. Karl felt that here at last was someone he could talk to. Especially his worry that as he was paid for by other people he must not cost them too much money.

'Then why don't you take the school certificate next December and go into the sixth form. It means you save a year. That's what I am going to do, come and join me.'

This was bold thinking. 'Do you think I could do it?' he asked.

'Of course you can, any fool can pass the certificate,' Ben said with that mixture of assurance and contempt that made him so hated among the boys. 'Look, all you have to do is to pick the right subjects. Your Latin is all right. English will be all right if you work at it, you will never do the maths so just leave it, do biology – if you pass that and Latin you will compensate for failing mathematics and you can take art; everyone passes in art, and then there is geography; well if you can't pass that . . .'

Karl was astounded by Ben's confidence and his wide knowledge of what could be done in the school. He even took Karl to see Steve who listened to what they said, then asked, 'Are you sure you want to do it? If you do that's all right, I will tell the masters concerned.'

Karl was becoming more confident and in lessons he would talk and even try to discuss things. Steve took him for religious instruction and they were always arguing about human motives. It seemed to Karl that self-interest was the only motive and whatever seemed otherwise was just a good smokescreen. Steve was shocked. 'Do you mean that no one ever does anything for anyone else?' 'Not unless there is something in it for them.'

Steve became cross and Karl was excited; this was like a chess game, if he made the right moves Steve became angry. 'You are nothing but a Machiavelli, Hartland,' he said, and although Karl had only read Machiavelli's name in passing he felt pleased that his ideas were like those of a Renaissance figure. It pleased him that an adult took his argument seriously enough to become irritated, but also that Steve did not use his authority to impose his point of view. It was like the house meetings; Steve got angry but always on equal terms; he showed that he saw things differently and he was not going to accept another view without fierce discussion; but he actually argued with his pupils; most other headmasters would have just ordered them about. Karl admired him for that.

As Karl grew more sure of himself he felt he could play about in the class like the other boys. This was a great luxury to him; and although he enjoyed it he was also scared, he remembered his German form master saying to him, 'A boy in your situation cannot afford to do things like that.' He was still 'in a situation', but it was a kinder one and the teachers seemed to tolerate a degree of misbehaviour that was really surprising to Karl, who thought that if he played up teachers he would no longer be thought a swot but as one of the boys. On the other hand he had to get his work done, so he stayed in the library late in the evening and walked back to the Edwards' house by himself. He would dream about Ann, and hope that they would meet, but when they did he could not say very much. Instead he carved her name on trees with his little penknife and composed letters he did not send.

On games afternoons Karl was eventually allowed to work in the garden. This was a blessed release. At first they had sent him to the playing field with boys of his own size, put a piece of wood in his hand and stood him in front of three sticks; he had lifted his piece of wood, which they called a bat, and a ball had whizzed underneath, someone had shouted 'out' and he was sent back to the pavilion. The next week he was with a group of smaller boys and the same thing happened until no team could be found willing to teach him the intricacies of the game and so he hid in the moat and waited until they had finished the game and packed up the things. Then he was allowed to go back to school to change for tea.

The games things were kept in the locker room, a room that on all four walls was covered with doors; each boy had a locker of his own. The doors had once been painted brown, but now they were scratched and had pieces of wood chipped out of them. Boys kept their extra food in their lockers, which they padlocked carefully, and much bargaining, arguing and swapping went on in the locker room. If a boy had something to give away he would shout 'quis' and whoever shouted 'ego' first got whatever was on offer; it might be a toy or a piece of bread or just a dirty sock. Karl was very conscious of not having extra food. In the evenings one had to fill up with bread and jam; Karl did not want to be thought a scrounger so he forced himself to refuse any offers from anyone who wanted to share his 'wealth' of fish paste or jam, because he had nothing to give in return and that would have made things difficult. In the house-meeting a boy proposed that all the parcels boys received should be shared out. 'Why should those who are rich,' he argued, 'have more to eat then those who are poor? Besides some people have parents who have a shop and they get tins of pineapple and things.'

Karl so hated the idea that he might be thought to be one of the envious 'have nots' that he argued for the rights of private property. Much to his own amazement he found he could get up and talk in the meeting because he had enough confidence in his English. Also there was a general acceptance of all contributions; no one was ever told that it was not his right to say what he thought, though there had been a gasp of horror and amusement when one of the youngest boys got up and said, 'Mr Chairman, I think Matron is a bitch.' Neither Tim, the chairman, nor anyone in the house could disagree with that sentiment but they offered the first-former advice on how to express himself in a more parliamentary fashion.

Karl was still treasuring the memory of dancing with Ann but could not find a way of meeting her again, nor of overcoming the danger involved in talking to Sandy's girl. But one day Sandy said to him: 'I know you are keen on Ann. I'm fed up with her. You can't do anything with her. I am taking Clicky out this Sunday, I bet I get a decent feel there.'

Sunday afternoon was the time for most amorous encounters. Karl wrote a note to Ann, and every evening after prep he rushed to his locker to see if she had replied. Yes, she wrote, she would be pleased to come for a walk and would meet him by the cinema on Sunday.

After lunch that Sunday he set out to meet Ann, accompanied by shouts from the smaller boys who leant out of the window and called 'Boy, oh boy, oh boy', and 'We know where you are going'. Karl felt embarrassed and quite proud. Ann was waiting and they walked over the golf course to a huge oak tree that had been struck by lightning and was quite hollow inside. They sat down and Karl took Ann's hand and kissed her. It wasn't a very good kiss, it went across her lips and he could feel a slightly damp nostril, but still it was a kiss and he felt a marvellous triumphant shout inside himself – 'I have kissed a girl' – and there he was. He did not know what to do next, but it was a nice contented feeling just to sit there and talk, and Ann told him about home, how she hated being in lodgings and how their landlady spied on her and she was sure that she did not get all her rations. And Karl told her about the nice Edwards and the dainty breakfasts which were the envy of all the boarders. Karl and Ann held hands until they came to the road and then they flew apart as they saw groups of boys hunting for something in the river. Karl promised to put notes in her books and they agreed to meet again next week. Then they parted.

Karl was greeted by the boys as he came into the school. 'Where did you get to?' Harry asked. Sandy was interested too. 'Any luck?' he asked benevolently. It seemed he had had a very satisfactory afternoon with the notorious Clicky. Karl did not really want to talk about it, also he suspected that a kiss half-way across the nose was not something that entitled him to a great deal of boasting, and so he allowed himself a happy and mysterious smile.

'Well,' asked Harry who seemed a bit cross, 'did she let you touch her tits? That's the least surely.'

'I am not saying,' replied Karl haughtily.

'In that case you didn't get anywhere.'

'Oh, yes I did, but I don't see why I have to tell everyone about it.'

'Oh yeah.'

After the fall of France the police came and took away the two refugee boys who were over sixteen. It happened without any warning. One morning Ben came up to Karl and said, 'They have taken all the older boys away.' Karl had missed being interned by just a few months, but now he had to register as an alien. He was given a grey registration book that had his photograph in it and he was told the rules: he was not to leave the town for longer than twenty-four hours without reporting to the police station, he was not allowed to ride a bicycle and he was not allowed to move beyond a radius of five miles. They did not take his fingerprints and the officials were friendly to Karl; they almost seemed to apologise for a set of silly rules not of their own making. As Karl did not have a bicycle and did not go for any long journeys the rules did not bother him too much, although he hated being known as an 'enemy alien'. He had to appear before a tribunal that was going to decide if he was dangerous as well as being an enemy alien. Steve told him about the tribunal and said, 'I'll come with you and make sure that someone stands up for you and try and stop this internment nonsense.'

They travelled to the tribunal together and Karl had to face a large man in a grey suit who smiled nicely and asked him how he liked it in England.

'Very much,' said Karl.

'Do you play cricket at school?'

'I try to, but it is very difficult.'

At this they laughed and a lady with a hat on asked Karl what he was going to do when he finished at school. Karl said that he would like to go to university, but that he wanted to go into the army to help in the war if that were possible.

'I hope you mean our army,' said the man with the gold glasses, and again they smiled and said he could go.

Steve took Karl to lunch and it impressed him that he allowed him to choose what he wanted and that he bought him wine and talked to him like a friend at a meal and not like someone in high authority.

'I think you will be all right. Interesting, I came in and said I wanted to say something in favour of Karl Hartland, and they said, "No, Mr Steven, we want you to help us to determine whether this boy is a threat to the country in this emergency or whether it is safe to have him running around free." ' Steve told Karl about Lytton Strachey, who had to go before a tribunal when he was a conscientious objector in the first war, and they said to him, 'What, Mr Strachey, would you do if a German attacked your sister, and Strachey replied, 'I would try to get between the two, your honour.' Steve laughed like anything at that story and Karl tried to, and said to himself it must be true that Germans have no sense of humour or else I would have laughed at that and meant it.

As a result of the tribunal Karl was allowed to go on as he was, but the other boys were deported to Australia. Ben said,

'Now that the seniors are gone you are bound to become a prefect much more quickly.' Neither Karl nor Ben regretted the departure of the two senior boys although the sudden arrest and the general panic that accompanied it was of course frightening. Steve was also accused of being a German sympathiser because he had allowed so many refugees to come to the school. Ben said it was a member of the staff who had reported him; many of the older teachers resented Steve with his new-fangled ideas and his nasty habit of bringing foreigners into the place. One in particular seemed to have it in for Ben and smacked him right across the face in a PE lesson. He was a tall man with a bristly, military moustache and he was in charge of the cadet corps. Every Tuesday the corps assembled, and the main activity seemed to be shouting and getting each other into straight lines. Even the smallest boys wore flat hats with visors; their uniforms did not fit very well and they carried huge rifles. The master in charge dressed up in a major's uniform and he had an impressive number of First World War medal ribbons on his chest. He carried a short cane which he pressed under his arm and he stood aside while the boys who were sergeants and corporals reported to him and saluted. On one occasion a group of boarders was watching the parade and suddenly the 'major' went deep red and rushed up to a boy, shrieking, 'Were you laughing at us?'

'Oh no, sir, we were just telling each other a joke.'

'You were not, you were sneering at the king's uniform,' and he really seemed about to hit the boy with his stick. He was so violent and out of control that the boys were seriously frightened, and then like an avenging angel Old Toss appeared, twitching fearfully but outwardly calm. 'Are you physically attacking one of my boys?' The two men stared at each other and both were shaking with rage and neither was prepared to give way until the major seeing that he was being watched by his 'men' decided to control himself. He turned away threatening that he would report the matter, particularly the unprofessional behaviour of a colleague.

'Hum hm, hm, you do that,' muttered Toss, and went away.

The boys were delighted, and Karl felt new admiration for Toss, who occasionally patted him on the head in an absent-minded way and said, 'Hm hmpf Karl.'

His eccentricity was such that Karl learnt a lot from him just because he never knew what to expect next. One biology lesson he made a joke, 'Ho hmph hm, Queen Elizabeth is in dock to have her bottom scraped.' Then he twitched, and convulsed his face, and the boys roared with laughter and he went on about the unequal distribution of protein foodstuffs. Another time Karl clashed with him in the library when Toss went over to him – 'Take this message to Matron, Karl' – giving him a piece of paper. Karl was irritated because he was working and he really did not like the thought of being a messenger boy, and so he said as politely as he could, 'Please, can someone else go, I am rather busy.'

'Hmph, now look here, you do as you are told and go.'

Karl felt weak in the knees but he decided to stand up for his rights. 'No, I won't go.'

'Look here, Karl, you will be in the army before long and you will have to obey orders, you can't just do as you please. Now off you go.'

'No I won't.'

Toss rushed off in a great state, muttering and humphing and hawking and Karl was scared now. He remembered his German form master again. 'In your situation, you can't afford to do that sort of thing' and his position at the school was not all that powerful or secure. Toss never patted him on the head after that, and Karl was less keen on biology, but he also had to admit to himself secretly that Toss was decent not to report him or to punish him. Most of his time was spent with Ben planning their school certificate work and making careful notes and learning them.

The invasion was expected at any moment. They saw London burning in the distance and Little Ted was optimistically talking about the effect the Home Guard would have on any invader. A pine tree moving in the wind covered and uncovered Venus on the evening sky, and the Home Guard turned out to catch the signaller on the hills. Karl wanted to join the Home Guard but they did not want aliens; he tried to get an interview for the air force but he was too young and the officer said, slyly, 'In any case we can't take the risk that the Germans get a present of a bomber, can we?'

Karl felt it was hopeless. How could he explain his position to people who could not tell the difference between a German National Socialist and a German Jewish refugee. In any case no one seemed all that bothered. The anti-glider ditches stood across the polo field but the anti-tank defences carefully stopped short at a fine flower bed, and the boys lay in the grass watching the fighters tracing fine white lines overhead in the sky. They went to see a bomb crater on the downs; they collected pieces of aluminium from a crashed fighter, and when he was alone Karl dropped a pair of dividers on a town plan. Each hole was a bomb crater, and he inked round the hole, imaging that he was bombing a German town. He read and learnt about Palmerston's foreign policy and did not understand a word of what he was doing, he learnt Latin translations by heart and in the end he took the examination quite calmly. Once he was the only candidate, that was for figure drawing, when he drew 'Knitting for Victory' – a nice lady in an armchair, and for good luck he put in a cat as well. For his English paper he wrote on 'Memories of Childhood', and described a Braque reproduction that was hanging on the wall in the library as his earliest childhood memory. He drew the eye and the nitrogen cycle in his biology paper and in literature he spotted poems by Wordsworth and Shelley and described *Gulliver's Travels* although he had never read it in English – but he had learnt the notes Little Ted had given to him.

Karl was walking to school with Harry earlier than usual. There was always a difficulty. If the boys went late, Little Ted went even later. He would not walk with them and they had to go ahead. This time Ben came running up to Karl. 'You have got the certificate, one distinction, five credits, two passes and a fail in maths. We can go into the sixth form now.'

Epilogue

Karl's father died in Theresienstadt concentration camp. The death certificate said he died of enteritis.

Grandfather Freudenberg died on the way to Theresienstadt, the trip was too much for a man more than eighty years old.

Aunt Cecilia and her mother Julia died in a concentration camp in Germany.

Uncle Julius died in a French internment camp. Aunt Flora escaped during the German occupation of France, went to Brussels and was hidden in a secret room by a Belgian colonel. One of her sons and his wife were liberated from Belsen but they were so weak they only lived for a few days after their liberation. Their two daughters tried to get to Switzerland but disappeared without a trace.

Cousin Joseph lives in Canada.

Mr Charc was called up in the German army, had to go to Russia but survived the war.

The Monds survived the war and Karl visited them in 1949.

Lutz, son of the 'other Hartlands' joined the American army and visited Essen as a GI. He now lives in America.

Uncle Eric died in Argentina.

Margot worked in a war factory, married and is now settled in the USA.

Karl finished school and later joined the army. He went to India and Burma during the war. Afterwards he went to university, taught for a time and is now a university teacher.

One of the gymnasium teachers wrote to Karl after the war and asked him to testify that he had never been anti-semitic.

The house in Lindenstrasse was completely bombed and the house in Alfredstrasse had a bomb in the front garden and the whole building collapsed. Karl saw it when he visited Essen in 1949. There is now a printing factory on the site.

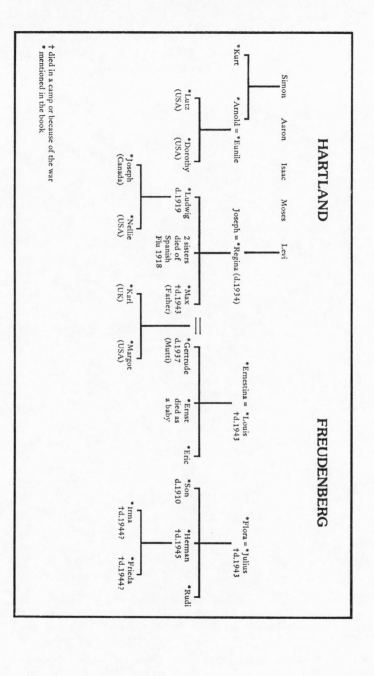

HARTLAND   FREUDENBERG

Simon   Aaron   Isaac   Moses   Levi

*Kurt

*Arnold = *Eunice

*Lutz
(USA)

*Dorothy
(USA)

Joseph = *Regina (d.1934)

*Joseph
(Canada)

*Nellie
(USA)

*Ludwig
d.1919

2 sisters
died of
Spanish
Flu 1918

*Max
†d.1943
(Father)

*Karl
(UK)

*Margot
(USA)

*Gertrude
d.1937
(Mutti)

*Ernst
died as
a baby

*Eric

*Ernestina = *Louis
         †d.1943

*Flora = *Julius
      †d.1943

*Son
d.1910

*Herman
†d.1945

*Rudi

*Irma
†d.1944?

*Frieda
†d.1944?

† died in a camp or because of the war

* mentioned in the book